Always Dreaming

Gaining Insights from the Metaphors of our Sleeping and Waking Lives

David L. Rivinus

©2015 David L. Rivinus

All rights reserved. No part of this book, in part or in whole, may be reproduced, transmitted or utilized in any form or by any means, electronic, photographic or mechanical, including photocopying, recording, or by any information storage and retrieval system without permission in writing from Ozark Mountain Publishing, Inc. except for brief quotations embodied in literary articles and reviews.

For permission, serialization, condensation, adaptions, or for our catalog of other publications, write to Ozark Mountain Publishing, Inc., P.O. box 754, Huntsville, AR 72740, ATTN: Permissions Department.

Library of Congress Cataloging-in-Publication Data

Rivinus, David, 1949 -

Always Dreaming: Gaining Insights from the Metaphors of our Sleeping and Waking Lives by David L. Rivinus

Suppose life could be taken at more than face value. Imagine seeing the individual events of our waking world metaphorically—like symbols in a dream. It is the idea that there is essentially no difference between the dream world and the world of our waking lives.

1. Life Interpretation 2. Dreams 3. Self Help 4. Self Discovery

1. Rivinus, David, 1949 – II. Waking Life Interpretation III. Dreams IV. Title

Library of Congress Catalog Card Number: 2014960305

ISBN: 9781940265148

Cover Design: noir33.com

Book set in: Mongolian Baiti & Candara

Book Design: Tab Pillar

Published by:

PO Box 754

Huntsville, AR 72740

800-935-0045 or 479-738-2348 fax: 479-738-2448

WWW.OZARKMT.COM

Printed in the United States of America

To Patti, with love and gratitude

(1933-2011)

An uninterpreted dream is like an unread letter.

—Rav Chisda—

(The Talmud)

TABLE OF CONTENTS

ACKNOWLEDGEMENTS

I would like to thank the following readers whose thoughtful suggestions improved early manuscript drafts in many ways. Penelope Adams, Vada Mossavat Adams, Mark Cohen, Beverly D'Urso, Verni Greenfield, Archie Hurst, Jeff Manthos, Doug and Karen Marman, Charlene Marchi, Adrian Martinez, Steve Otto, Chris Rivinus, Nina Rivinus, Patti Simpson, Stephen and MaryLou Taylor, and Phuong Thao Tran.

Jennadelle Palmer was an early mentor whose classes on dream interpretation greatly influenced my thinking.

I extend my gratitude and respect to the dreamers whose stories and insights over the years have informed and enlightened me.

Special thanks go to Raf Schnepf for his beautiful illustrations.

Finally, I am particularly indebted to my editor, Adrienne Casco, whose tireless insistence on clarity and focus influenced the final shape, content and tone of this book in numerous, important ways.

INTRODUCTION

The path to an understanding of waking life as a dream began with my work as a teacher of children at a mental health clinic, and continued with further research into the field of psychology.

Suppose life could be taken at more than face value. Imagine seeing the individual events of our waking world metaphorically—like symbols in a dream. How would that affect how we live, what decisions we make, who we associate with? This intriguing idea was one I began to ponder in earnest as a young man while working in the education department of an outpatient mental health clinic. I had recently graduated from college with a minor in psychology, and worked at the clinic as a teacher of children with emotional problems and brain disorders.

In the often intense setting of this kind of school environment, the person who learns the most is the teacher. The clinic's staff of social workers, psychologists and psychiatrist all made themselves available when questions arose. We teachers took liberal advantage of their willingness to assist. The staff also encouraged continued education, occasionally suggesting a book, or recommending a seminar or workshop. For me, it was training in the trenches, under fire.

This took place in the late 1960s and early 1970s—before congress enacted a national policy in regard to special education—and it was a particularly rich time in the field of psychology. The giants—Freud, Adler, Jung—had long had a monopolistic hold on the imaginations of therapists. Now they were being challenged by other ideas. New voices like those of Skinner, Pavlov, Rogers, Erickson, Harlow, May, Maslow, Wolpe and Piaget were being heard, and their work was taken seriously. Among many changes, there was a concerted effort to turn psychology into a science that could be held accountable.

I remember reading a massive and fascinating study by Truax and Carkhuff. These two authors concluded that patients who participated in years of Freudian analysis were less likely to recover from their problems than if they involved themselves in no therapy at all. This understanding would be pivotal in my own search for a psychological approach. In general, those of us involved in the clinic's education program read voraciously. We experimented with a wide variety of techniques through role-play, and tried to find what worked most comfortably and effectively in this new smorgasbord of clinical options.

In the middle of this heady time, I attended some workshops run by psychologists who were devotees of Fritz Perls, one of the founders of the Gestalt therapy movement. I was immediately captivated. The techniques offered a more streamlined alternative to years of expensive psychoanalysis, and I was especially moved by the effectiveness of the Gestalt approach to dreams. I bought a copy of Perls' book, *Gestalt Therapy Verbatim*, and couldn't put it down. For years it was my therapeutic bible. That was when I began working with dreams myself, initiating dream interpretation sessions with friends and family members. I soon expanded my exploration to include others as my confidence and understanding grew.

Because of my unorthodox clinical training in general, I had few qualms about experimenting with dream analysis techniques. I was often my own guinea pig, keeping a dream journal and waking myself up in the middle of the night to record dream experiences. I started with the dream analysis techniques as I had been learning them through Gestalt workshops. The Gestalt approach was to use role-play to help the dreamer become more aware of symbols. But I soon came to see that reliance on this technique—primarily designed to assist people in crisis—was often as much an impediment as a help. People who simply had dreams to relate didn't necessarily need to participate in such an extreme and exhausting activity.

I began to devise a simple and gentler method, one that involved no role playing at all. It necessitated only a minimum amount of instruction to learn. It could be done anywhere—in the comfort of an easy chair, in bed, while riding in a car. It didn't require any specialized training. I found that dream analysis could be made simple as well as extremely effective. It didn't need to be complicated with lists of symbol definitions, Freudian psycho-sexual theory or the archetypical characters who populate the collective unconscious.

At the same time, I latched onto a concept that was only hinted at in Perls' writing. It is the idea that there is essentially no difference between the dream world and the world of our waking lives. Through my own work and experimentation, and while using this new dream analysis method, I discovered that when one understands one's waking life as if it were a dream and then acts upon the personal insights that are revealed by that understanding, the world takes on a whole new meaning.

We are all familiar with dreams. They are often disjointed. Their scenes shift and move about without order. They lack consistency. Their plots can be confusing and illogical. But this can also be a quality of our waking lives; we all have been involved in incidents while awake that seemed to make no logical sense.

I decided to try an experiment. What would happen if I applied these new and simple dream analysis techniques to the startling or unusual events of daily life? I subsequently learned that one can successfully analyze an event from waking life exactly as if it were a dream, plus I saw that this could be a significant source of healing.

After working with both the new dream interpretation method and a radically different way of looking at waking life, I wanted to see how generalized this method and these ideas were. I have some facility in four European languages and began taking my dream work on the road to other countries with specific questions in mind. Was my method limited to those sharing a particular view of life? Limited to a minimum level of education or a common upbringing? Was it effective only in English? Only in the United States?

I have now facilitated dream workshops in Germany, Austria, Switzerland, France, Italy, Canada, Mexico and the U.S. In addition, with the help of a translator I have worked with Asians, especially individuals of Chinese and Japanese descent. Although I have never kept count, I have certainly facilitated the analysis of many hundreds of dreams. I have worked with both children and adults. Through it all, I have come to realize two things. First, I believe that dream symbols are the vocabulary of a universal language. Second, I realize that the simple method I have devised works effectively at interpreting both the dreams we have during sleep and the events of our waking experiences. This was true of dreams and waking experiences I helped analyze in every culture I visited.

The idea of interpreting events of our waking life as if they were dreams is likely unexpected and perplexing, however we can learn much from those unusual, startling, repetitive or scary incidents that sometimes haunt our days. These kinds of experiences are almost universally accepted as literal events, but they can also be seen as dream symbols.

When we take the time to interpret waking events as symbols, they function as a way to help us understand ourselves in more depth, thereby allowing us to gauge the direction and health of our lives. The personal stories contained in this book, when seen in the context of this unusual way of viewing life, will allow the reader to understand and appreciate the insight and wisdom such analysis can provide.

Many in the field of mystical, esoteric learning have referred to this uncommon life view: "What you see in the world around you is a reflection of yourself; you create your own universe." That is a widely held spiritual adage especially in Eastern philosophies. But it is unusual to find an author who teaches a simple way to convert that understanding into an effective tool for daily living. It is my hope that the techniques presented in this book will offer access to a realm of life that few have discovered, especially in the West, but which can have an indelible, constructive influence on our health and well-being.

If we take advantage of the symbolic information that can be discovered in the events of our waking lives—this in addition to the symbols of our sleeping dreams—we can make a profound shift in our thinking and behavior. This idea, as startling as it may seem, is one that we will thoroughly explore in the pages to follow.

NOTES TO THE READER

- Throughout the text, many dream examples are shared, my own among them. These stories are indispensable to learning the interpretation techniques presented. However, only a handful of powerful dreams will be given prominence; the rest will act solely to illustrate a point being made within a relevant chapter.
- Where the anecdotes and incidents of others are used to illustrate concepts, the privacy of individuals has been respected. Names, locations, occupations and genders have been changed. For the purpose of clarity, the text in several monologues and conversations has been streamlined.
- Dream stories and concepts have been developed sequentially across chapters. Therefore, it is suggested that the book be read chronologically.

PART ONE:
THE INCIDENT

Part One examines how unusual incidents in waking life can be interpreted as dreams.

1

A harrowing real-life experience with an automobile becomes a dream with a poignant message.

The phone call came while I was at work; that's what surprised me. I had been volunteering my counseling services for years, helping friends and acquaintances interpret a peculiar type of incident, one that happens to a person during the day, one that tends to leave an upsetting impression. Sometimes these events can be alarming and it is not unusual for the participant to be shaken. Still, no one had ever experienced such consternation that they felt obliged to interrupt me at my job. When I heard the story, I understood:

A friend of mine—Austin — had calmly been doing errands. He'd backed his car into an empty space in a strip mall parking lot and had gone about making his purchases. When he was done, he'd returned, started his engine, put his car into gear and removed his foot from the brake pedal. Before he'd even touched the accelerator, his car, seemingly of its own volition, had lurched forward at such a speed that, before he could gather his wits and react, it had careened the length of the small lot, crashed through a three-foot retaining wall, bolted across a sidewalk and ended up, broadside, in the middle of the street. Fortunately, there was neither foot nor vehicular traffic, and the most significant casualty was the poor wall that was now marred with a wide gap. Understandably, Austin was rattled.

The auto mechanic's eventual assessment was simple enough. The small computer that regulated the various functions of the car's cruise control wasn't working correctly, and the vehicle had simply tried to accelerate to what it erroneously determined was a "preset" speed. Frightening!

Austin was understandably upset. He would have been perfectly justified in registering a complaint to the automobile manufacturer or even pursuing a lawsuit. But he had recently gained a different understanding of these kinds of events. Although he was angry, Austin was interested in analyzing his daytime experience as if it were a nighttime dream. Rather than the two of us working ourselves into a lather bemoaning the shoddy construction of cars or commiserating about the unfairness of life, our goal was to examine each element of his mishap as if it were a symbol—a visual image that stood for something broader than its literal meaning. We began with the overall theme of his experience: Austin had been running errands. We took the word "errands" and decided to treat it metaphorically, as if the word stood for something beyond a short trip one might take to perform a task. From there, we went on to other words that described his experience, words like "parking lot," "car" and "retaining wall." In each case, we wanted to step back from the strictest meaning of the word and try to understand it in a more general sense. What follows is how our conversation began.

David: So Austin, let's work on the dream symbols. The first one, as I understand it, is "errands." You were running some errands, right? Tell me about errands.

Austin: Well, they're like routines, maybe chores. They're things you have to do on a regular basis to keep order and make your life run smoothly.

David: (writing down his responses) Tell me about parking lots.

Austin: It's where you temporarily put your car when you need to leave it for a while. It's a space you borrow—not really anything you own.

In similar fashion Austin and I worked our way through every moment of his unpleasant adventure. We took the key words he used to describe his mishap and focused on each one as if it were a metaphor. I would bring his attention to the word by asking the neutral question, "Tell me about it." That would usually lead to a kind of free-association definition like those above, in which Austin would try to pinpoint the essence of what those words meant to him.

This did not always go smoothly. The emotional impact of the incident was so strong that he sometimes had difficulty, and I was obliged to help him re-focus on what was important.

David: Tell me about your car.

Austin: (still upset) Oh man! That pile of junk!

David: Well that's probably part of the answer, but it's not really what I'm looking for. Let me see if I can help direct you better. Pretend I'm five-years-old, and am asking you a question. I come to you and say, "Austin: Tell me what a car is."

Austin: I'm talking to a kid?

David: A five-year-old, so your answer needs to be simple.

Austin: (pause) A car's the thing you use to bring you from one place to another. It's the thing that takes you where you want to go. And, when it's working right, it moves you around only when you want it to. But sometimes... Man!

David: (laughing) Thank you, that's better.

Austin and I were looking for the essence, the core, the most basic meaning of each of the words we chose to analyze as dream symbols. As long as he was emotionally invested in his calamity, his answers were unhelpful. But when I obliged him to respond to me as if I were a small child, he both distanced himself from his visceral reaction and forced himself to give the simplest answer he could think of. It was exactly what I was after. We kept going until we had worked our way through the entire incident.

David: Now, tell me about three-foot retaining walls.

Austin: Well, they're a barrier. But not really a serious one. They're more for psychological reasons than anything. I guess you could say they're there to define spaces.

David: Tell me about racing across a parking lot.

Austin: Wow! Out of control. Lurching forward. Really scary.

David: Good. We're almost done. Tell me about the middle of the street.

Austin: Well, a street is a pathway—or maybe "avenue" is a better word. You use it to get to your destination. Streets are vital, and you're supposed to be in the middle of them. But if you end up broadside, I guess it could be dangerous.

We were done. We had methodically worked our way through each facet of his unsettling automotive episode and pretended that it was nothing but a series of symbols, metaphoric images that we had picked apart in an effort to discover the core of their "meanings."

What I was going to do next was to retell the story of his car incident back to him in a different way, with two changes. First, in my retelling of his event, whenever I got to one of the words we had picked out as symbols, I would omit that word. Instead, I would substitute his explanation of the symbol. I would try to use his exact words. So, for example, rather than saying, "I am running errands," I would use the same words he spoke when he described running his errands: "I am going about my routines, chores, the things I do on a regular basis to keep order and make my life run smoothly."

Second, since we were going to pretend that this incident was a dream, we were going to follow one of the tenets of dream analysis. As a rule in dreams, each symbol represents some aspect of the dreamer himself. I was going to repeatedly remind him of that. So instead of saying, "I am running errands," I would say, "There is a part of me that is doing my routines, chores, the things I do on a regular basis to keep order and make my life run smoothly." In this way, I would remind him often that the action was unfolding inside himself. I would insert phrases into the narrative that would repeatedly focus his attention on that idea. By the time I finished retelling his story in this peculiar way, it would reveal a different kind of plot. It was one I hoped would be more about Austin, himself, and far less about physical things like cars and parking lots.

David: I'm going to describe your incident right back to you. You know the routine, right?

Austin: Yes.

David: Instead of using your symbols, I'm going to substitute your definitions for them. And the whole time I'm going to keep reminding you that it's all about you. Ready?

Austin: Yeah.

In the following retelling of Austin's dream, I have also included the original symbols in parentheses.

David: There is a part of me that is sitting in a space within myself that is temporary (parking space). I don't really own it. I'm busy with my personal routines, chores. I'm working at things in myself I have to do on a regular basis to keep order in my life (errands). Suddenly, without warning, the part of me I use to take me where I want to go—to take me from one place to another place (car)—pulls me forward. It's scary. It's out of control. It's only supposed to happen when I want it to. But this time, Man! This part of me forces me to burst through another part of myself that is a barrier (wall). It's not much of a barrier, really. It's more psychological than anything, mostly there to define spaces. Anyway, I find that I've thrust myself right into the pathway—the vital avenue—(street) I use to get me to my destination. But I find that I'm facing crossways—broadside—which could be dangerous for me.

When the incident was retold in this way, the story seemed coherent and also seemed to deliver a meaningful message. No longer about cars and walls, this version of Austin's experience seemed to be describing changes occurring within himself. It implied that, despite some of his own resistance, he was evolving in ways that might, eventually, "get me to my destination." However, the story, as it emerged through metaphor, also seemed to contain a warning. There was something about being "broadside" in the middle of this "pathway" that "could be dangerous."

Remembering that each symbol represents some aspect of the dreamer himself, was there anything Austin could gain from turning his attention to the "communication" his "dream" seemed to be delivering? What might he learn about himself from revamping his story in this fashion? The next step was to analyze the incident's "message" to ascertain if it had relevance to anything happening in Austin's life.

2

Austin perceives a connection between his car incident and a troubling conflict in his life.

Austin and I had dissected his shocking and worrisome automotive experience and had come away with a radically different view of what it might be about. The next step was to investigate if the incident's "message" had relevance to anything happening in his life.

While there are many exceptions, I have found that most dreamlike occurrences of this type seem to point to a looming crisis or shift in attitude in one of three common arenas: work, home, or one's social environment. I suggested these possibilities to Austin, and asked if the "message" might speak to anything occurring in one of these three areas.

David: Ring any bells?

Austin: Geeze! (pensive silence)

David: If this "dream" were mine, I'd ask myself if there was anything going on in my life that involved a sudden change or shift, something that feels out of control or uncomfortable.

Austin: Well, the first thing I'm thinking about is what's going on at work.

David: OK.

Austin: I get the feeling there's change happening, but you can never tell with those guys. They claim they're going to do all this great stuff for you, but then they start double-talking and putting up obstacles.

David: Obstacles? You mean like cinderblock walls?

Austin: (laughing) I hadn't thought of that.

David: If you're loony enough to buy into the idea that a strip mall and a car are both parts of you, it shouldn't be too much of a stretch to see your managers at work in the same way, should it?

Austin: No.

When one begins to observe life in this fashion, one begins to see patterns. One becomes cognizant of this dreamlike, metaphoric quality all through the fabric of one's daily existence. Now, suddenly, Austin became aware of two metaphors—cinderblock walls and intransigent managers at work—that seemed to be about barriers. That there were now two symbols implying obstruction added weight to their importance, and they became even more difficult to ignore.

Why were the barrier symbols there with such consistency, and perhaps even more importantly, who was responsible for putting them there in the first place? Who was constructing metaphoric walls—cinderblock or otherwise—in Austin's life?

David: So, Austin, who's the mason here? The one who's cementing all the cinderblocks together?

Austin: Me, I guess.

David: OK. And, if this dream were mine, I'd wonder if I had some mixed feelings about all this: You talked about mixed messages being delivered at work. The symbols in your dream seem to be saying that you want to break through some barriers but are feeling that the shift would put you out of control.

Austin: You got that right.

David: Yet from the symbols, it sounds as if change, perhaps a career change—since this is happening at work—is where you'd really like to be in your life. Am I right? I mean all that stuff about ending up on the pathway that takes you to your destination?

Austin: Yeah.

One of the predictable qualities of these kinds of real-life "dreams" is that they seem, fairly consistently, to have two aspects. First, they present the "dreamer" with a description of a conflict, one that has been growing and evolving in his life, but one that the dreamer has probably been ignoring or resisting. Second, they imply, and sometimes directly suggest, a solution to the dilemma.

David: So how do you keep from feeling out of control and ending up facing crosswise to the traffic?

Austin: That's always what I do. I get an idea of how I'd like my life to be. I start going in that direction, and then I shoot myself in the foot.

David: You mean you put up barriers?

Austin: Yeah.

David: So maybe those managers at work who are getting in your way are really only doing what you're telling them to do.

Austin: What do you mean?

David: Well, you just told me that you put up barriers whenever you get an idea that you want to follow. Those managers are just helping you be who you are; they're helping you "shoot yourself in the foot" to use your own phrase.

As a Western culture, we are unaccustomed to thinking in this way. We tend to believe that external influences are only that, namely, unsolicited obstacles that life puts in our way. We think we have to battle them as if they were an enemy unfairly forced upon us. We feel maligned and victimized. Austin, up to this moment, would have agreed. He would have considered his work situation and automobile accident to be part of life's arbitrary indignities that we are obliged to contend with, even though we never asked for them. On the contrary, I was suggesting to Austin that they appeared in his life precisely because he did manifest them through his own attitudes and behavior patterns.

David: Austin, how do you stop your managers at work from being punitive?

Austin: I'm not sure, but I think you're going to tell me I have to change myself.

David: Well, let me ask you another question. What have you done so far that has helped your situation at work?

Austin: Not much.

David: So what do you have to lose by trying a different approach?

Austin: Nothing.

David: OK.

Austin: (pause) You know the weird thing is, I've known that for a long time. I don't even know why I've put it off so long.

David: We all do that.

Austin: (shaking his head) Weird!

David: Austin—Here's fifty bucks that says if you make changes in yourself, things at work and with your car will change, too.

Austin: You think so?

David: I just put fifty bucks on it.

3

Austin makes personal changes, and his life at work radically alters.

During our extended conversation, Austin told me that, at work, he was feeling increasingly marginalized—on the one hand trying to behave appropriately as an employee, but on the other, sensing his work environment closing in around him, restricting him and causing him to feel increasingly unimportant. He said he found the substance of our session peculiar, but also strangely reassuring. He was ready to try the ideas we discussed.

In the weeks that followed, what happened at work took him by surprise. He began to assert himself more and no longer went out of his way to be accommodating. He thought, perhaps, that his managers would ease up if he presented himself with greater authority. The opposite happened; they became increasingly belligerent, and his work environment grew nearly intolerable.

At the same time, a colleague noticed an ad in a newspaper for a position that seemed ideal for Austin. Austin applied, was accepted, and is now much happier. His comment was revealing: "The whole series of events seemed orchestrated. There was no doubt that I was being forced out of one job, but it was as if I was being steered from a bad situation into a wonderful one."

These days Austin is careful to be assertive, and whenever he finds himself reverting to his old habit of "putting up barriers" by quietly subverting his own plans, he makes a course correction.

There may be those who question this approach to dealing with life's unusual waking experiences. Perhaps Austin's car episode was simply an accident, a fluke. But I take a different view. In more than 25 years of working with peculiar, bizarre, sometimes frightening incidents—like Austin's—I would strongly argue that such messages are not coincidental, but appear in the dreamer's world to teach and enlighten. They are arresting, forcing the participant to pay attention and tend to deliver important information.

Over the years I have been amazed at the coherent communications that emerge from the most irrelevant-seeming events in people's lives. Despite varied cultures, language constructions and views of life, I have rarely come across an example that didn't reveal some significant insight. What's more, I find them fun. What are symbols, after all, but another language—that of the metaphor? I am as confident today about betting $50 on the results as I was all those years ago when a shaken, bewildered Austin knocked on my door.

4

Unusual events in one's life—like Austin's incident—have significance, and can be categorized and interpreted as "waking dreams."

I began with Austin's experience because it is one of the more dramatic examples of an unusual event that occurred while the dreamer was awake. It demonstrates that much can be learned about life when one applies the same analysis procedures used for sleeping dreams, to waking occurrences.

The unusual, daytime experience that Austin encountered is what I call a "waking dream." Among the hundreds of events that occur in any given day, it is the unusual event that will be carefully examined in this book. Although most of us don't have problems with a cruise control, all of us have experienced similarly strange and seemingly inexplicable incidents in our lives. These "waking dreams" tend to have at least one of three qualities:

1 They are shocking.

2 They are bizarre.

3 They are repetitive.

Later in the book, after some important principles of dream interpretation have been explained, we will give close scrutiny to each of these qualities as expressed in the dream-like occurrences of people's daily, awake lives. Nevertheless, it is helpful to offer brief, introductory examples now. The following three unusual daytime events—waking dreams—were brought to my attention by individuals, like Austin, who wondered if there was significance to them beyond their face value.

A shocking event A young woman entered her apartment building late one evening, looked down the somewhat darkened hallway and was scared out of her wits to see a man with his arm outstretched in her direction, holding a pistol that was aimed directly at her head. In her shock, it took her a moment to realize that the figure was a mannequin, insensitively and inappropriately set up as part of the upcoming Halloween celebrations.

A bizarre event An overdue paycheck finally arrived, and the recipient, in a hurry to deposit it, held onto it while he went into his lavatory to run a comb quickly through his hair. In the process, the check slipped out of his hand and dropped into the toilet.

A repetitive event A businessman knew that he could cut ten minutes off his commute if he exceeded the speed limit along a certain stretch of roadway. He had been doing it for years without incident and couldn't understand why, suddenly, he'd been ticketed three times in the last few weeks.

As this book progresses, we'll examine other waking dreams like these, hopefully presenting them in a new light and offering techniques for understanding them at a deeper, more comprehensible level.

As a side note, it was a friend who, in the early 1980s, introduced me to the term "waking dream." It happened as I was only beginning to understand the concept. When I explained the phenomenon to her, she was struck by the dreamlike quality of these events. They seemed disjointed and surreal. Though the vast majority of them were happening in broad daylight with the participant fully awake and cognizant, there was an out-of-control, fantastical quality to them that reminded her of the process of dreaming. The term was so appropriate that I began using it right away, not knowing if it was original or if someone else might have applied it in this or in another context.

It was only as the idea for writing this book was suggested, that I discovered that the term "waking dream" has been adopted by other authors—for a variety of meanings and purposes[1]. Despite that, the term is apt, so I continue to use it. It accurately describes and neatly distinguishes this phenomenon from the more commonly known and analyzed "sleeping dream," to which I intend to give equal consideration.

---

[1] The earliest use of the term "waking dream" that I found in English is Mary Watkins' landmark book Waking Dreams (1988). There is an earlier book in French entitled Le Réve Eveillé (The Waking Dream). Both those documents address topics only peripherally related. Other authors cited in the bibliography who use the term "waking dream" for a variety of meanings are Ray Grasse, Mike Avery, Zoe Newman and Catherine Shainberg.

5

The precedent for the waking dream includes examples from the past and present.

I had been working with sleeping dreams for years. Discovering the phenomenon of the waking dream was a surprise to me. As part of an exploration to see how closely related the two types of dreams were, I first experimented with my own unusual daytime occurrences—my own waking dreams. I then turned my attention to other scholars, philosophers, artists and thinkers to learn if anyone else had heard of this. How naïve could I be? It seemed that, in all of recorded history, the only cultures not aware of the waking dream were those of the West since the industrial revolution. This book will give equal time to both types of dreams. Nevertheless, it is instructive to take a glimpse at the waking dream's widespread acceptance throughout history in other cultures. The waking dream's historic documentation tends to be through hearsay and fiction, but one can still get a good sense of the prominence and importance of the concept in earlier times.

In this chapter we will explore it in ancient Rome, eleventh century Tibet, and through a Shakespearian character. We will also give mention to great Western thinkers in modern times, such as Carl Jung and Fritz Perls, who have bucked the general trend and worked with the phenomenon.

Jung, for example, published a paper in 1952 called *Synchronicity—An A-causal Connecting Principle*[2]. In it, he argued that there is something in life that deliberately creates what most people regard as coincidence. Further, he felt that there was a connection between the "coincidence" of certain types of odd, illogical events and the "messages" they are designed to deliver to those who witness or experience them. He offered the example of a woman who was the wife of one of his patients during the early decades of the twentieth century. In casual conversation she mentioned to him that, at the deaths of her grandmother, and later her mother, sizable flocks of birds had gathered on the roofs of the houses where these two women were dying. Years afterwards, when her husband was

---

[2] Jung, C. G; Synchronicity—An A-causal Connecting Principle. Princeton, NJ: Princeton University Press, 1969.

brought home following his sudden collapse from a heart attack, the wife—unaware of this medical incident—was already in a high state of agitation because she had just watched a large flock of birds alight on their home.

There is no logical connection between birds and death. Similarly, there is no demonstrable link between malfunctioning cruise controls and a man's (Austin's) hesitation when it comes to asserting his wish for a more meaningful type of employment. Yet in both these cases there appeared to be an association between a physical event and a seemingly unrelated message that the witness of the event needed to receive. In Austin's case, he understood the message after participating in a simple dream interpretation technique. Jung offers no similar analysis, but the consistent reappearance of birds whenever the woman was obliged to grapple with the death of a loved one, establishes a pattern beyond mere coincidence.

This same juxtaposition of an unusual event and a message being delivered has been understood on one level or another for thousands of years. Depending on the culture and civilization, it has been used in various ways and referred to by many names. The ancient Roman understanding of these phenomena—which that culture referred to as omens—is lucidly described by the English historian, Adrian Goldsworthy, in his book, *Life of a Colossus*, a scholarly biography of the Roman general and statesman, Julius Caesar. What follows are excerpts from Goldsworthy's description of Caesar's last day, just before he was famously assassinated on the Ides of March. The entire account is full of the warnings of soothsayers who have made predictions of Caesar's demise based on their readings of the remains of sacrificed animals. As in Austin's case and in the flocks of birds that Jung's acquaintance saw, there is nothing logical that connects the entrails of dead animals and the murder of a Roman emperor, yet these Roman prophets gave great credence to the relationship. What's more, their predictions seem to have been accurate.

From Life of a Colossus:

Our sources are filled with prodigies warning of the death of Rome's most powerful man. One of the most famous [of them] claims that on the night of 14 March Calpurnia [Caesar's wife] suffered a nightmare in which she is variously claimed to have seen either the pediment of the house collapsing or that she was holding his murdered body in her arms. Then the morning sacrifices on the 15th were repeated several times, but the omens were always unfavourable. [Underlining added.] Caesar is supposed to have been surprised because his wife was not normally given to superstition...

None of the sources suggest that [Caesar, on his way to the senate where he was stabbed to death,] was in any way suspicious and he cheerfully called out to a soothsayer, who had previously warned him to fear the Ides of March, in an exchange so familiar from Shakespeare—'The Ides of March are come.' 'Aye, Caesar, but not gone.'[3]

A general sense of foreboding seems to have arisen from both a sleeping dream of Calpurnia's and from reading "omens"—waking dreams. One soothsayer apparently even got the date correct. It is well documented that Roman (and other) prophets understood the concept of what we are calling the waking dream, the idea—as Jung expressed it—that there is something in life that connects events or objects and seemingly unrelated messages. As such, it was possible for these fortune tellers to pay attention to one kind of thing and, from it, learn about something completely different.

Can one take these soothsayers' analyses at face value? Our Western view would be that their methods are invalid; the Romans strangely came to rely on a superstitious method of gobbledygook to try to make sense of their world.

Curious, that the most advanced superpower of its day, one that had all but conquered the known Western world and had brought a degree of order and highly engineered physical structure to its territories, should fall prey to such a frivolous practice! That is the Western attitude. But those in the West who hold this opinion would be in the minority of world belief throughout history; the Romans were not alone in their reliance on this waking dream phenomenon.

In Eastern cultures waking dreams have been understood for thousands of years. As a young man, the great eleventh century Tibetan sage, Milarepa, was living and studying with his guru. The young student wanted permission to take a break in his studies and

---

[3] Goldsworthy, Adrian; Caesar; pp. 506-507.

visit home for a while. Milarepa approached his teacher as the latter was sleeping and chanted his request using the quasi-sung poetry that was the style of his time. His guru awoke and gave permission, justifying his decision by pointing to the various signs and omens he was witnessing at that particular moment. These were simple phenomena he was paying attention to: being asleep, seeing the sunrise, his wife bringing food. But the guru saw great importance in them.

... if thou desire to go, I grant thine appeal. If thou count on coming back here, know that finding me in sleep when thou didst come to address me is an omen that we two shall not meet again in this life. But the rays of the rising sun shining upon my dwelling-house is a sign that thou wilt be a shining light amongst the Buddhist hierarchies, and that thou wilt glorify the Faith. And the sun's rays enhaloeing my head is a sign that this Sect of meditative [Buddhism] will flourish and spread far and wide. Further, [my wife] bringing in the morning meal just then showeth that thou wilt be sustained by spiritual food.[4]

One needn't look to ancient Eastern history for a cultural understanding of the waking dream phenomenon. Several years ago, when I was living in New England, I was late for a doctor's appointment due to inclement weather. After apologizing to my stately Chinese physician, Yang Zhou, I offered a brief explanation based on the waking dream. I did so lightheartedly, so I was surprised at his response.

I told him that my delay was due to the nearly-impassable roads, making it difficult for me to reach my source of medical help. I wondered if this omen—this waking dream of slick roads—might be suggesting that my viral infection would be particularly "slippery" and difficult to "grab hold of" and cure. Dr. Zhou quietly sat back in his chair, looked pensive for a moment and finally said, "It is rare to speak with a Westerner who understands this idea." He took my remarks seriously.

I think Dr. Zhou would be pleased to learn that, although rare, there are those in the West who know of the waking dream phenomenon.

---

[4] Evans-Wentz, W. Y; Tibet's Great Yogi Milarepa; p. 160.

The irascibly brilliant German-American psychiatrist, Fritz Perls, who worked a great deal with sleeping dreams, was once asked point blank, "Is it possible to use an unresolved life situation as if it were a dream and work on it in the same way?" His response: "Yah. Just the same."[5] Perls knew all about it. And so much is communicated in this simple exchange that we'll give Perls and his Gestalt movement more attention later in the book.

Shakespeare understood the concept of the omen—the idea that one can read meaning into irrelevant-seeming signs and events. One of my favorite plays is *Hamlet*. It is a superb and brilliant drama, an emotional and physical bloodbath told in exquisite iambic verse. The tension starts almost from the first line and doesn't let up for over three hours. In the midst of all this excitement and turmoil, there is one curiously calm scene which many scholars consider the pivotal moment of the entire piece. In this long, violent play, it's a pause of utter peacefulness which Shakespeare makes even more poignant by writing in straight prose. There is no action, no metaphor, no poetic verse. It's simply a conversation about a fencing match Hamlet is supposed to participate in, which seems innocuous enough on the surface but which is somehow enveloped in a cloud of foreboding. Hamlet's buddy, Horatio, is offering to get Hamlet out of the event. And Hamlet, in his matter-of-fact response, rebuffs him. He makes it clear that there are no accidents in life, that he must follow through with whatever it is that circumstances have presented to him, even if he senses danger. To do otherwise is to "defy augury"—disregard prophesy—and that's impossible. Perhaps one can postpone the inevitable, but if the sign has been given—through an omen—then there is no escaping it.

Horatio continues to press Hamlet, urging him to avoid the fencing match: "If your mind dislike anything, obey it: I will forestal their repair hither, and say you are not fit." And Hamlet's adamant reply is:

Not a whit. We defy augury. There's a special providence in the fall of a sparrow; if it be not now, 'tis to come; if it be not to come, it will be now; if it be not now, yet it will come; the readiness is all.[6]

---

[5] Perls, Frederick S; Gestalt Therapy Verbatim; p. 125.

[6] Shakespeare, William; Hamlet; Act V, Scene II, lines 130-131.

According to Hamlet, one must pay special attention to omens. Something as insignificant-seeming as the death of a small bird has deliberately been arranged by the universal powers-that-be and can be used to understand what life has in store for us.

Hamlet was talking about a bird. So was Jung's acquaintance. Similarly, animals in general play a profound role of guidance in Native American culture. The concept of the totem is central to the beliefs of many tribes. It is the idea that certain animals—each of which carries a special metaphoric significance—will appear to clans or individual humans to deliver a "message" of protection or advice when such is needed.[7] Over the years, as I have helped people work with their waking dreams, there have been numerous, extraordinary examples of animal encounters, so this is hardly a phenomenon indigenous to American Indians.

One such example of an animal encounter occurred after my elderly father died in 1998. He was an outdoorsman—a naturalist, ornithologist and hunter. Had he lived in different times he would (and should) have been a biologist, but there were few available careers in that field when he was a young man. Instead, he became a diplomat and an amateur naturalist who compiled impressively long lists of the birds he had sighted all over the world.

Following his death, the last ceremony his family performed was the spreading of his cremated ashes along his beloved Patuxent River in Maryland. When we were done, we left the state park along a narrow road—not much wider than a single lane. I was driving one of several carloads of people. I don't know what first caught my attention, but I happened to look up to my left and there, running parallel with us, was the most magnificent stag I have ever seen.

Mind you, while I was growing up, my father made a valiant effort to share with my brothers and me not only his love of hunting, but also of the outdoors and wildlife in general. As a pubescent male who wanted nothing more on a Saturday morning than to sleep until noon, I cannot tell you the number of times I was hauled out of bed before dawn, to go traipsing through yet another frozen and godforsaken hinterland to catch a fleeting glimpse of some noble beast that my father would be thrilled to share with me. Bucks are elusive at best; one can track for days without finding one. In my brief stint as a hunter

---

[7] en.wikipedia.org/wiki/Totem

I have seen several, but to have such a superb animal come to me was literally breathtaking.

He was close enough that I specifically remember the flexing of his powerful shoulder and haunch muscles as he ran. Had I not been so dumbfounded, I surely would have counted the points on his impressive antlers to determine his age. Nevertheless, I was certain that he was one of the local princes of his species, if not the king. What a marvel! What an honor!

I have little concept of how long this buck stayed directly beside our caravan—perhaps 30 or 40 yards—before he suddenly veered off and disappeared as magically as he had manifested. It was long enough for everyone in the car to gasp in awe, and for someone to quietly comment, "That's a salute from your dad." And for me to respond just as simply, "Yeah. I know." No one disagreed.

Is this wishful thinking? coincidence? superstition? poppycock? happenstance? Certainly our culture as a whole would think so. Yet we would be in the minority when compared with civilizations throughout the ages. The vast majority of cultures all over the world continue to embrace the concept of the sign or omen—the waking dream. In addition, some of the greatest minds of our own time and culture agree.

In Austin's case, it didn't take him long to act on the "message" brought to him courtesy of his malfunctioning cruise control. He interpreted his mishap as a waking dream and shifted his attitude. That, in turn, dramatically changed his life. He began a new, more suitable career. He also made a concerted effort to approach his work from a new perspective, one that has made him much happier.

His experience is only one of a long line of occurrences that acknowledges a connection between seemingly-random events and the attitudes of witnesses to those events. Making the effort to understand those connections can have important, life changing benefits. The understanding need not be elusive or bewildering. It comes from the simple, straightforward method of dream interpretation that we will explore in ever greater detail as this book progresses.

6

Five steps of a dream interpretation technique are discussed in detail.

By the end of Chapter 3, we saw that Austin had arrived at an understanding of his waking dream's message. He did so after participating in a simple dream interpretation technique. The purpose of this chapter is to present the five steps of this technique using another waking dream. It will help the reader understand and possibly experiment with these five steps while continuing to read. The steps will come up repeatedly throughout the book in regard to both waking and sleeping dreams.

Simply stated, the five steps are as follows:

Step 1 Relate the dream.

Step 2 Isolate the symbols.

Step 3 Interpret the symbols as metaphors.

Step 4 Retell the dream using and owning the metaphors.

Step 5 Explore the dream's relevance in one's life.

Step 1: Relate the dream.

This is straightforward. The dreamer simply shares a dream. This often involves telling some sort of bizarre dream plot of illogical-seeming events. Sometimes the dreamer is emotionally invested, especially at first, and the narration can be animated. Usually, it is recommended to tell the story in the present tense. Doing so has a way of keeping the experience current in the dreamer's mind. Curiously, it also has a calming effect because the dreamer has to think a moment in order to tell the dream in a new way. This tends to distance him from his emotional charge.

We introduced the concept of the waking dream with Austin and his cruise control. Now, we'll offer another waking dream. This incident happened to the dreamer on a summer afternoon, again, while she was wide awake.

I am out for a walk. I see a plum tree that is full of beautiful ripened fruit. Because I am looking up into the tree, I miss seeing an irregularity in the pavement. I trip and fall flat on my face. I think to myself, "I'm lucky. I'm bruised, but nothing is broken."

That was the waking dream in its entirety. Now it was incumbent on the dreamer to dissect the dream, break it down into its various components in order to understand it in a different way. This dissection process would begin in Step 2.

Step 2: Isolate the symbols.

Isolating the symbols takes some practice. Symbols can be anything. Some of them will be apparent immediately; others will be subtler. Obviously, "things" in a dream (nouns) are symbols. Taking a glance at the waking dream above, the following are all symbols: a walk, a plum tree, beautiful ripened fruit, a pavement irregularity.

But it is important to look beyond nouns. Feelings, actions, thoughts, even a strong sensation during a dream are all important to consider. In our dream sample above, the following are all vital elements of the dream: the actions of tripping and falling, the thoughts, "I'm lucking" and "I'm bruised," and the dreamer's final assessment that "nothing is broken."

The dreamer and I discussed these and other possible symbols and came up with the following list.

A walk

A plum tree

Beautiful ripened fruit

Miss seeing

Pavement irregularity

Trip

Fall

Face

I think

I'm lucky

I'm bruised

Nothing is broken

In general, if you are working by yourself on a dream, it is helpful to write the dream down. It often happens that words spoken in passing seem unimportant. However, they stand out when seen on a written page.

As an alternative, one of the best ways to work on dreams is to partner with someone. Another point of view and insight can be invaluable, especially when one is first learning the technique.

Above all, it is important to consider the entire dream. There is a tendency to think, "Oh well, that part of my dream isn't the main point; I'll just skip it." This can happen especially if the dream is long. But more often than not, ignoring a part of the dream leads to a skewed interpretation.

Step 3: Interpret the symbols as metaphors.

The topic of metaphors is one that we will examine thoroughly in Chapter 10. For now, suffice it to say that a metaphor is a word—often a visual image—that has a meaning broader than its literal definition. A good example is the word "food." Its literal meaning is: an edible substance that you ingest to help you maintain life; it is nourishment. But the idea of food as nourishment can be associated with issues that go far beyond one's digestive track. "Food for thought," or "food for the soul" are both abstract ideas that are more easily understood when the word "food" is associated with them. In this context, the non-literal meaning of "food" becomes a metaphor.

Step 3—interpreting the symbols as metaphors—like Step 2 above, takes a little bit of practice. However, most dreamers surprise themselves at how quickly they catch on. This step is also the most fun because it is like a game.

Finding the metaphoric essence of a word involves reducing that word to its most basic meaning. In my dream interpretation sessions, I start with the neutral directive, "Tell me about it!" This noncommittal phrase allows the dreamer to answer in his unique way. That is often enough to trigger a useful response. In the case of the dreamer who tripped and fell, I started this process by referring to her first symbol. I said, "Tell me about a walk." And she replied, "A walk is a pleasant way to get exercise." Her response was a cross between a definition and an act of free association in which she also expressed her attitude about walking. In later steps, when we reassemble her dream, we'll see that her phrase "a pleasant way to get exercise" will become prominent, and the specific word "exercise" will be understood metaphorically rather than literally.

Sometimes, in responding to the "Tell me about it!" prompt, a dreamer will give an emotional reply instead of a definition. While it might be an honest response, a detailed, less impassioned explanation is more likely to contain a metaphor central to the dream's message. We saw this with Austin in the earliest chapters of the book. He was so upset with his automobile that, at first, he couldn't divorce himself from his own anger and frustration. His initial response to my suggestion that he tell me about his car was to say, "Oh man! That pile of junk!" While "junk" can certainly be a metaphor, the emotional nature of his answer prompted me to press further, albeit gently. I asked Austin to respond to me as if I were a small child: "I'm only five-years-old. I don't understand what a car is. Tell me about a car." You may remember that part of his thorough, more helpful response to this second prompt was, "A car's the thing you use to bring you from one place to another. It's the thing that takes you where you want to go." That second reply was a definition full of metaphor.

The dreamer who tripped might also have given an emotional response to the "Tell me about it!" prompt, such as: "Tell me about a walk." "Oh, I just love taking walks!"

In the above hypothetical response, while it might be useful to know of the dreamer's association with pleasantness and walks, there is no definition that could be interpreted as a metaphor. As a dream facilitator, I would want to probe gently to elicit one. The "small child" prompt would work well in this scenario.

Another effective approach is to pretend that the questioner is an alien from another planet. "I'm a Martian and I have no comprehension of things on earth. Tell me about taking a walk, and please do so in a way that I can understand." Suddenly confronted with having to explain a walk to an alien, a person usually gives a more thorough and useful response, such as, "Well, a walk is a form of exercise—where you move your body in order to stimulate your muscles. This is important for healthy survival. Some forms of exercise involve a lot of work which can be unpleasant. But taking a walk is an activity that I enjoy."

Now let's go back to the woman who fell, and see how she responded to the "Tell me about it!" prompt in regard to all the symbols in her waking dream. In each case, her answers immediately follow the prompt, and her symbols are underlined for greater clarity.

Tell me about <u>a walk</u>.

A walk is a pleasant way to get exercise.

Tell me about <u>a plum tree</u>.

When I think of plum trees, they always remind me of the expression, "That's plum!" as in "That's really desirable."

Tell me about <u>beautiful ripened fruit</u>.

Delicious, Sweet. Juicy.

Tell me about <u>miss seeing</u>.

I wasn't watching where I was going.

Tell me about a <u>pavement irregularity</u>.

A pavement is where you walk, and it is supposed to be smooth. But every once in a while there is a deformity in the surface that can be dangerous.

Tell me about trip.

It's when you stumble.

Tell me about fall.

You go crashing to the ground, and you can hurt yourself.

Tell me about a face.

It's the part of you that's the most recognizable. It's also the part that has your most important sensory features—like your eyes and ears and nose and mouth.

Tell me about think.

I'm pondering. Ruminating. Assessing.

Tell me about lucky.

Fortunate. Blessed.

Tell me about bruised.

I'm sore. I'll have marks, but I know it's minor and temporary.

Tell me about nothing broken.

That would have been worse. It would have meant doctors and hospitals. I would have been incapacitated. It could even have been permanent.

While most people would have given similar answers to those above, I suspect, as you were reading, that you might also have sensed your thoughts going in a different direction from time to time. That's the beauty of this approach to dream interpretation. Some responses are common to most of us. Others are so much a part of the human psyche that they are archetypical. But still others are completely individualized. The result is an interpretation that is unique to the person who had the dream, either waking or sleeping.

Step 4: Retell the dream using and owning the metaphors.

In Step 4, the dream gets told again, but with two changes. First, in place of the symbols, the dreamer's responses to the "Tell me about it!" questions will be substituted when retelling the dream. As an example, let's revisit the first sentence the dreamer said when she was telling her dream. She stated, "I am out for a walk." I then prompted her by saying, "Tell me about a walk," and she replied, "A walk is a pleasant way to get exercise." In retelling the dream during Step 4, the first sentence would change to something like, "I am involved in a pleasant way to get exercise."

Second, during the retelling of the dream, we will not only use the metaphors that were revealed in the definitions, but we will do so in a way that the dreamer takes responsibility for them; the dreamer owns them. While dreams can be about anything in life, it is a tenet of dream analysis that dreams are always about the dreamer. In the decades that I have facilitated dream interpretation, I have never known of an exception. The dreamer, in owning the metaphors, personalizes the message. This is done by repeatedly inserting a simple phrase into the narrative. The phrase can be, "There is a part of me that..." It can also include an occasional statement such as "inside myself." In the case of this dreamer, in retelling the above dream, instead of saying, "I am out for a walk," we would say something like, "There is a part of me that is involved in a pleasant way to get exercise."

Now let's retell the entire dream. When you read what follows, think metaphorically:

There is a part of me that is involved in a pleasant way to get exercise. As I am exercising, I see a part of myself that's "plum;" it's really desirable. This part of myself is delicious. It's sweet and juicy. But I am so taken with this part of me that I stop watching where I am going inside myself. Where I am going inside myself it is supposed to be smooth, but every once in a while there is an irregularity that can be dangerous. Inside myself I stumble and go crashing to the ground where I might hurt myself. I fall right onto the part of myself that is the most recognizable—the part of me that contains my most important sensory features—my eyes, my ears, my nose, my mouth. I find myself pondering, ruminating and assessing inside myself. I feel fortunate and blessed because even though I am sore and know that I will have marks, they are minor and temporary. It could have been worse. It could have meant dealing with the doctors and hospitals inside of me. It could even have been permanent.

Suddenly, a bizarre, upsetting incident—accidentally falling flat on one's face while admiring the ripe fruit of a plum tree—is transformed into a coherent, poignant message. There is logic, and there seems to be a clear warning about a dangerous preoccupation.

Step 5: Explore the dream's relevance in your life.

The final step in the dream interpretation process is simply to answer the question, "What is this dream about?" To begin the exploration, I tell dreamers that their dreams are most often providing commentary on one of three aspects of their lives: their work, their home environment or their social setting. Sometimes pinpointing the dream's relevance can involve some minor sleuthing, although often the dreamer knows right away what the message is referencing. In the above instance, I initiated the dialogue with a simple prompt:

"If this dream were mine, I'd ask myself if I am becoming overly complacent in some aspect of my life. I'd wonder whether I was paying attention to some clues about a 'rough spot' that could cause me to 'lose my balance.' Does that resonate in any way?"

The dreamer needed no further nudging; she said she knew exactly what the dream was referring to. She told me that, after 17 years of living alone following a divorce, she had met a man she thought was a compatible mate. After months of dating, they had decided to move in together. She was in love. She was happier than she had been in years. But she was beginning to imitate a pattern that had been an old, destructive one in her life. She had begun to surrender completely to her new relationship, quietly ignoring her own needs for the sake of the partnership. She said the "pleasant exercise" inside herself was the sense of joy in the co-habitation. The "delicious fruit" was her feeling of being in love with her new mate.

But she knew that the success of their relationship would depend on her functioning as a whole person—not surrendering "the most recognizable part" of herself. She knew that her failed marriage, 17 years prior, was due, in large part, to her unwillingness to express her own needs. The direction her marriage had taken had finally become so intolerable that she needed to terminate it. She realized that her preoccupation with the "delicious fruit" of her new affair was going to lead to her "crashing to the ground" as she lost the use of her "most important sensory features."

In our subsequent discussion, it also became clear that her dream contained an assessment of how deeply the potential crisis had progressed. Assuming she acted promptly on the dream's warning that she maintain her own sense of self, the result would be "soreness" and a few temporary "marks." But there would be no need for her to call upon her own, inner medical staff of "doctors and hospitals." There had been no "permanent" damage.

The dream interpretation techniques presented above have been given in ordered fashion, each step explained in detail. This dream of the woman falling while looking at a plum tree was a waking dream. It occurred while the dreamer was going about the normal business of her life. She found herself the "victim" of a bizarre occurrence. But rather than feel sorry for herself or bemoan the unpleasant flukes of existence, she chose to analyze her experience as if it were a dream, and as a result, was given the gift of an important insight.

Let's now direct our attention back to Step 5. During this step—in which the dreamer worked toward discovering the dream's relevance—I initiated a dialogue by offering suggestions about what the dream might be trying to convey. I deliberately began with the phrase, "If this dream were mine..."

This is a practice that is especially important during classes when multiple participants are commenting on a dream. When there is a lot of discussion, it is vital that ideas and suggestions be offered only as possibilities to be considered. They must never be delivered as indisputable interpretations. Sometimes, in the excitement of a moment of discovery, the person offering the suggestion forgets and gives an opinion too adamantly: "Oh I know! Your dream is saying that..." Even when stated with the most well-meaning of intentions, this is presumptuous, and in extreme cases, is an intrusive violation of the dreamer's private thoughts. For that reason, I routinely urge anyone who is assisting in a dream interpretation to preface his comment with a phrase implying that he is only making a suggestion. "If this dream were mine..." is a simple and effective way to accomplish that goal.

We will examine this concept in detail in Chapter 28 when we delve more deeply into the process of dream interpretation in group settings. However, the reader may have noticed that this practice has already been implemented, not only above, but during Chapter 2 with Austin and his cruise control. It will also come up frequently throughout the rest of the book.

With a more in-depth understanding of the five step dream interpretation process in mind—including the important protocol of using the phrase "If this dream were mine..."—we will continue to witness examples of insight through dreams. We will encounter the five steps again in the next chapter where we eavesdrop on a young man and his wife as they struggle to understand the meaning of the husband's sleeping dream about a mistress.

PART TWO:
IT'S NOT WHAT IT SEEMS

Part Two examines some of the pitfalls of taking dreams—both sleeping and waking—at face value. It begins to make practical use of the dream interpretation techniques introduced in Chapter 6.

7

A sleeping dream about a mistress is less upsetting when understood metaphorically, using the five-step dream interpretation technique.

In Part One, Austin chose to examine his cruise control woes as a dream—a waking dream. Fortunately, Austin had previously worked with dreams metaphorically, and our session went smoothly.

That is not always the case. The idea of considering life events as symbols is a concept radically different than what we are taught in the West, one that is often difficult for a Westerner to grasp. That was the case with a married couple, Linda and Jeremy, who were referred to me by a mutual acquaintance.

We are about to eavesdrop on my dream interpretation session with them. I will be using the five-step technique introduced earlier and will indicate each step as we proceed.

Step 1: Relate the dream.

This couple is sitting, facing me across the kitchen table. Jeremy is slouching, arms folded across his chest, with a cap pulled low over his eyes. Linda is seated upright and stiff. A dream of Jeremy's has upset her—a sleeping dream. It involved a woman whom Jeremy identified as being his mistress. Linda is alarmed.

Jeremy: I don't remember it all.

David: That's fine. Even a piece of it can help.

Jeremy: Well, this was a couple of nights ago. In the dream I was in some kind of room, and the feeling I had was that it was formal.

David: The room was formal?

Jeremy: Yeah. I mean, not like a bedroom or a kitchen or anything. And I'm looking at this woman who is sitting on a couch, I think. I mean, she looks really comfortable, like she's not about to move. (pause) And I guess this is the part that's got Linda shook up. I'm looking over at this woman—who's blonde—and I'm thinking to myself: She's my mistress. (pause) And after that, the only thing I remember is looking for the door so I can leave. But I can't find it.

David: Good. (still writing) Have you ever worked on dreams before?

Jeremy: No.

Neither Linda nor Jeremy had ever thought much about their dreams, and now that one had made a dramatic impression on their lives, they were receiving it with great solemnity. Part of me wanted to suggest that they relax a bit. Sleeping dreams about lovers—including ones involving extra-marital affairs—tend to be instructive, but they're rarely about something that threatens a marriage—at least not directly. Since I had only recently met Linda and Jeremy, I decided it was better to talk them through the dream as expediently as possible.

I started by explaining how dreams work. I said that they speak in their own language, a language that is somewhat different than the one we use in common speech, but one that is easy to learn. I told them that our job was to act as translators. Anything that seemed important in the dream—a thing or an action or even a feeling—anything at all that left an impression—was to be taken seriously as a symbol. It was the language of these symbols that we would need to understand. Also, it was important to interpret all of the symbols that the dreamer could remember; otherwise, part of the communication would be left out, and the overall meaning would be distorted.

Step 2: Isolate the symbols.

I explained that, while I had been listening to Jeremy, I had been writing down some words that he used to describe his dream, the symbols I thought were key to the message. I showed him the sheet of paper which I had divided in half, lengthwise down the middle. On the left side, I had written the important words, leaving lots of space between each symbol so that eventually I could go back and fill in Jeremy's explanations on the right. This is what I wrote:

Formal room

Blonde woman

Couch

Not moving

Mistress

Looking for the door

I suggested that it was probably a mistake to take these words at face value. Dreams could sometimes be taken literally, but the majority of them communicated in symbols. It was now our job to figure out what Jeremy's dream was trying to tell him. I explained that the next step was for me to try to help Jeremy do exactly that.

Step 3: Interpret the symbols as metaphors.

The process was the same as the one I used with both Austin and the woman who fell while looking at a plum tree. I would ask simple, non-leading questions to discover what Jeremy thought about each of the symbols.

David: I'm going to ask you to talk about each one of your symbols, and I'm going to write down what you say. We'll start with the first one, which is "formal room." So, Jeremy, tell me about a formal room.

Jeremy: Tell you about it? What do you mean?

David: Start with whatever comes to your mind. If I think I need something more from you, I'll ask.

Jeremy: Well I guess if a room's formal, it's different than, like, a TV room or a "rec" room where you can just be yourself. Here it was more like you had to watch your manners—you couldn't quite relax.

David: Good! Tell me about blonde women. (Linda snorts a laugh.)

Jeremy: The first thing that comes to my mind?

David: Yeah.

Jeremy: I, uh. I had a blonde girlfriend once.

David: OK. Can you tell me about it?

Jeremy: Well, I guess you could say she was really beautiful. But then it was all downhill from there. (Linda laughs again.)

David: Good. Tell me about couches.

Jeremy: What I remember was that it looked really comfortable, and she wasn't about to move.

David: Tell me about mistresses.

Jeremy: Well, that's the thing that's so weird about this dream. I know guys are supposed to think that having a mistress—you know, having an affair—is really exciting. But I've never been like that. I think it would be mostly a pain. You'd spend all your time just trying to stay out of trouble.

David: Tell me about looking for the door.

Jeremy: You know how dreams are, kind of murky sometimes. I'm looking all over for the way to leave, and I can't find it.

David: Nicely done! Especially for your first time.

Jeremy's explanations of his symbols were detailed and full of metaphors. They would be useful in the eventual retelling of his dream. Here is how my paper looked when I finished writing:

formal room: have to mind my manners and can't quite relax and be myself.

blonde woman: beautiful at first, but all downhill from there.

couch: really comfortable, she's not about to move.

mistress: a pain, spend your time trying to stay out of trouble.

looking for the door: can't find the way to leave.

Step 4: Retell the dream, using and owning the metaphors.

As we saw with Austin, and later, with the woman who fell while looking at a plum tree, Jeremy's own explanations of the symbols would be substituted for the symbols themselves in the retelling. Sometimes, if the symbols in a dream seem particularly disjointed, retelling the dream while using these explanations can involve a verbal juggling act. For the most part, however, it is impressive how the "story" emerges on its own.

In retelling Jeremy's dream back to him, I was going to use as many of his own words as I possibly could. Further, I would remind him that the dream and, by association, each of the symbols in the dream, was part of himself. This is what I said to him:

David: Jeremy, if this dream were mine, I'd say that there's a place inside of me where I have to mind my manners and I can't quite relax and be myself. And sitting there inside of me is a part of myself that looks beautiful at first but turns out to be "all downhill." This part of me acts really comfortable and shows no signs of leaving... (laughter) ... And the thing is, though this is supposed to be attractive to a guy like me, it's really a pain. It complicates my life, and I seem to spend a lot of time trying to stay out of trouble, trouble that I make for myself. I keep looking for a way out, but can't ever seem to find it.

(a few moments of silence)

Linda: You mean his dream's not about a woman?

David: Doesn't seem to be.

Linda: Even though there's a blonde in it?

David: I'd guess probably not.

This session with Linda and Jeremy was far from over. But already one of the first objectives—that of easing Linda's discomfort—had been accomplished. In addition, some principles of dreams and their peculiarities had been demonstrated. First, Linda's concerns resulted from a literal interpretation of the dream. Like so many attempts to take dreams at face value, it turned out to be erroneous. Second, Jeremy's dream, which he had when he was fast asleep at night, told a story about himself that highlighted a circumstance that needed his attention—one that we will examine closely in the following chapters. Finally, the technique for unlocking the message hidden in Jeremy's dream was no more complicated than what was demonstrated here; anyone can learn how.

So far, I had taken this couple through four of the five steps of the dream interpretation technique. Now, we were about to turn our attention to Step 5 which examines the dream's relevance in the dreamer's life.

8

Jeremy and Linda explore the implications of a non-literal interpretation of Jeremy's "mistress dream."

In the last chapter we left Jeremy and his wife, Linda, pondering a dream about a mistress. We had progressed through four of the steps involved in dream interpretation, and now it was time to turn our attention to the fifth and final one.

The couple had arrived in a tense mood, concerned that the dream's plot was to be taken literally. As our discussion progressed, the two were beginning to relax. They started to have an inkling that this dream might be about something less threatening than an extramarital affair.

The shift in Linda's demeanor was especially fun to watch. She had invested energy in her role as the wounded spouse—worried that her husband's dream was a sign of infidelity—and now the curtain had suddenly come down on her performance. At first she wasn't sure how to deal with the emotions of relief on the one hand, and on the other, a sense of indignity over having expended energy on a non-issue. Besides, she wasn't at all certain she could put her trust in what was, to her, an unfamiliar and unorthodox way of looking at dreams. But it didn't take her long to work past that ambivalence and to absorb the new understanding.

Step 5: Explore the dream's relevance in your life.

It was time to turn our attention to the events and circumstances of Jeremy's life to see if we could find a connection between the dream's "message" and something troubling him in his daily affairs. As stated earlier, there are usually three arenas of conflict that dreams highlight: the work environment, the home and the dreamer's social life.

David: Jeremy, if this dream were mine, I'd ask myself if there was something in my life right now that was acting like a mistress—seemingly beautiful and presenting itself as a good idea, but turning out to be trouble, something that you can't seem to get away from.

Jeremy: Well, like I said, I don't have any interest in finding a girlfriend.

David: Yes, I understand that. But I think one of the things we began to discover as we worked through the symbols is that this dream probably doesn't have anything to do with women. The mistress is just a metaphor for something else in your life that seemed attractive at first, but then became a burden. Can you think of anything at all that seems to be a hassle, one that doesn't ever go away, a real aggravation?

Linda: You mean it can be about something that's not a blonde, not a love affair?

David: Yes. And, in fact, it probably is about something that has nothing whatsoever to do with intimacy. It could be something at your job or with your friends or even with your house.

Linda: The armoire!

Jeremy: The armoire?

Linda: You're always complaining about it.

Jeremy: I don't understand how that could be.

It turned out that Jeremy was a woodworker and an antique furniture restorer. About half-a-year prior to our meeting he had agreed to refurbish a valuable historic armoire. It was a handsome piece passed down through several generations of a single family, and so in addition to its monetary value, there was considerable sentimental investment in it as well. Jeremy had felt honored to work on it, but it had turned into an ordeal. He soon realized that the job was much more extensive than he had thought—or contracted for—and, to make matters worse, the work wasn't progressing smoothly. Little glitches would arise necessitating extra steps which translated into time and money lost. This, according to Linda, was his blonde mistress, the lover whose romantic allure soon disappeared but who showed no signs of leaving.

It took Jeremy a minute or so to make the connection. When he did, the relationship between furniture and amorous liaisons seemed obtuse to him.

I responded to his doubts by telling him about others who have dreams involving lovers. One friend in particular, Anne, has periodic dreams of being in affairs. These dreams are consistent with one another in the sense that they tend to begin with her entwined in a passionate embrace, literal or implied, and usually end with a feeling of guilt on her part because, in fact, she is a happily married woman. I explained to Jeremy that I had worked with Anne in the same way I had taken Jeremy, himself, through the symbols, asking her to "tell me about" each one. At first she had been mortified especially when she was obliged to discuss her sexual desires as they were expressed in these dreams. But when our sessions were over, she was delighted and enormously relieved, because her dreams, like Jeremy's, had nothing to do with either unfaithfulness or sex.

Let's follow Anne through this process for a while longer before returning to Jeremy. Like him, her understanding evolved in increments, and her realizations helped Jeremy shed light on his own circumstance. They will also help the reader appreciate Jeremy's dream from a broader perspective.

Anne is one of the hardest working, most diligent people I know. She gets an enormous amount accomplished, for her family, for her community and for herself. She is much in demand. But, as such, she has a hard time engaging in anything that might be considered frivolous, unimportant play. Taking a gorgeous summer afternoon off to go for a walk along a beach, for example, is difficult for her. She tends to feel that her time could be spent more constructively elsewhere, and it is easy for her to become lost in her work because she loves what she does.

When she and I worked through the symbols, that was exactly the scenario that emerged. In her own definitions, her husband—with whom she is deeply in love—is associated with her sense of wholesome commitment. So when she "cheated" on him in her dreams, she was temporarily opting to ignore her obligations, no matter how noble they were, for the sake of sheer pleasure. As we both agreed, in regard to her work, maybe ignoring her obligations wasn't such a bad thing to do once in a while.

I asked Anne if she would mind keeping an informal journal. I wanted to see if there was a juxtaposition between when she had this particular type of dream and when she needed to make choices between work and play. Whenever she remembered such a dream, I asked that she pay special attention to what had been happening in her life during the days immediately leading up to it. Was she feeling torn between work and pleasure?

We probably kept the experiment going for no more than four or five dreams over a period of months, but the results certainly supported this thesis, and by then she had learned a whole new way of dealing with her conflict. Instead of being a threat, her erotic dreams were now a constructive reference point. They alerted her to the fact that she was feeling a sense of ambivalence. They allowed her to step back and look at the particulars of any specific conflict of this nature, and they gave her the option to make a detached, calm decision about it. The result was that she began to play more. Far from being a detriment to her obligations, she saw that this new-found liberation actually helped because she was more relaxed and refreshed when she did attend to her commitments.

All this I explained to Jeremy. I also emphasized again the concepts we had discussed from the moment he arrived: Dreams are not what they appear; the symbols in them should rarely be taken literally. The emotional impact they have on us—often including a profound sense of guilt, fear or misgiving—is there primarily to make us remember them. In fact, the most unsettling dreams we have are often those that point to the greatest constructive changes we are in the process of making.

As he listened, Jeremy, like Linda, started to distance himself from his initial concerns over dreaming about a blonde mistress, and began to explore the possibility that his experience was about something he hadn't yet considered. He gave more serious attention to Linda's idea that, more than any other issue in his life at the moment, he was, indeed, troubled over his seeming enslavement to this piece of furniture. As we discussed the matter further, his descriptions of the armoire began to include more metaphoric phrases, even though Jeremy was unaware of doing so. He referred to it as "a really beautiful piece" that had become "a chain" around his neck, one that wouldn't go away.

I suggested to Jeremy that, since he was now more aware of his conflict, he could take steps to correct the situation. We discussed ways that he might approach the armoire's owners again, to renegotiate the terms, or ways that he might pace his work so that this one project didn't monopolize his time. Even in the course of our one session together, I became aware of a developing calm and constructive cooperation from Jeremy and Linda, one that was a far cry from the roiling mood during the first moments of our encounter. They knew they had work to do—a potentially unpleasant circumstance they had to confront and correct. But they had become conscious of what, specifically, had been bothering them—Jeremy's "enslavement" to the armoire, and Linda's obsession with the dream mistress. They knew the steps they needed to take to bring closure to the whole issue.

9

The suggestion is made that Jeremy's conflict with the armoire is a waking dream, one that is delivering the same message as his sleeping dream about a mistress.

What had transpired up to this point with Jeremy and Linda was typical of dreams and the way they are dealt with in a formal interpretive session. This is especially true in regard to sleeping dreams which are generally viewed as subconscious expressions of a circumstance in the dreamer's world. Sleeping dreams inwardly reflect what is going on outwardly in our lives at any given moment. A friend of mine likes to say, "Dreams are your own personal State of the Union message." They frequently become prominent enough to warrant our attention when a change in our status quo causes discomfort. One of the comments I am fond of making when a dreamer has finished working through symbols is, "If this dream were mine, I'd ask myself what has been going on in my life during the last few days." The idea is to find clues to the dream's reason for existing by searching through the events and concerns that have most riveted the dreamer's attention in the recent past. Jeremy and Linda had identified those clues to their own satisfaction. Indeed, they now found themselves motivated to make changes and to explore possible solutions to their problem.

Although they had accomplished a lot in this session, I wanted to find out if I could introduce Jeremy to a deeper understanding of life, a more profound way of viewing existence. I talked to Jeremy at length about how waking life by itself can be viewed as a dream, a waking dream.

David: One way of looking at your own dilemma is to see that you had one dream and one dream only: You dreamed about a blonde mistress and she was a symbol for an armoire.

Jeremy: Yeah, I guess so.

David: But another way to look at it is to see that you had the same dream twice. The first time you had a dream, and in it, the symbol was a blonde woman. Then you had a second dream—during the day—and this time the symbol was an armoire.

Jeremy: You lost me.

David: Well, let's go back to our earlier conversations. When we started, you described the blonde mistress as being "really beautiful" but in your dream, you couldn't find the door to get away from her. Right?

Jeremy. Yeah.

David: OK. Just now, when we were talking you said—and I'm pretty sure I'm using your words here—the armoire was "a really attractive piece" that has since become "a chain" around your neck, something that you find burdensome and want out of your life. Did I remember that correctly?

Jeremy: Yes.

David: You used different words, but aren't those ideas about the armoire pretty much the same as the beautiful blonde mistress who was hard to get away from?

Jeremy: Maybe. But one was a dream and the other's my work.

David: That's right. One was during the night while you were asleep, and the other is during the day. But they're similar.

Jeremy: (pause) I don't understand this at all.

I certainly could appreciate Jeremy's frustration. He was new to dream interpretation of any kind. Introducing the concept of the waking dream at this point was unfamiliar and confusing. Further discussion might have clarified the idea, but our session was already a long one. I dropped the subject, and this relieved couple went their way.

In the West we tend to view what happens at night in our sleep as different from what goes on during the day while we are awake. The idea that there is a close link between the two facets of our lives can be new and strange. For this reason I didn't push Jeremy any more on this issue, but further explanation will clarify one of the core ideas of this book.

Typically, Jeremy's dream—a sleeping dream—would be viewed as a symbolic expression of a situation taking place in his world. His dream would be considered an imagined metaphoric representation of something that was bothering him in actual life. The mistress would be seen as an illusion—a figment of Jeremy's imagination—and the armoire would be thought of as a reality since it was an important physical object in his world.

Now let's take a leap and examine Jeremy's experience from a new perspective—the one I briefly introduced to Jeremy himself. Let's start by taking the above concept (that the sleeping dream is a symbolic expression of a real-life situation), and then apply it to what I suggested to Jeremy was a companion waking dream about an armoire.

Jeremy came to understand that his dream symbol of a mistress was representative of an aggravation at work, an annoyance that he was now determined to change. As far as Jeremy was concerned, the cause of the problem was a contract he had negotiated with a client. With his new insights, he understood that this contract needed to be modified.

Although Jeremy's insight was useful to him, I saw things differently. In the last minutes of our session, I suggested that his sleeping dream and his frustration with the armoire were two versions of the same experience—two separate dreams. One of them happened during the night while he was asleep and the other during the day while he was awake. From my perspective, the contract that Jeremy was now so anxious to change was, in fact, secondary. What the dreams—now plural—were asking of Jeremy was to look at something within himself—perhaps an attitude or a life view—that was acting as a hindrance to his general functioning in the world. I suggested that the mistress and the armoire were exactly the same symbol, and both of them were about something else having to do with Jeremy's attitudes and perspectives on life, something that he hadn't yet examined. I proposed that the armoire (and the negative feelings associated with it) might be seen as a dream symbol all by itself, a symbol that might reveal some inner distress—one that we might have explored had our session continued.

The idea that there is far less difference between our waking lives and our dream world is a concept that is difficult for us in the West, but one that has long been recognized in the East. Even for those

through this sort of metaphoric mix that our dreams communicate with us. Let's revisit the above example restated as a sleeping dream:

In my dream, I'm out of doors in the middle of a storm. There doesn't seem to be any rain, but there's a lot of wind. I'm talking on the telephone, except that it's not a cell phone even though I'm outside. The phone has a wire that is connected to a thick vine that is loaded with ripe grapes.

Then the scene shifts and I'm in a theater. I'm in the wings, and I'm about ready to walk onto the stage. But I have to go through some sort of a doorway, and I notice that the door's threshold is really high. I realize that I'm actually going to have to leap over it to get onto the stage. What's more, lying on the floor, right in front of the doorway is a pistol which is partly covered with the lid of a frying pan. I'm nervous because I don't want to jump and accidentally hit the pistol. But I figure out that, if I approach the door's threshold from an angle, I can miss the gun. Finally, I back up, get a running start, and like a broad jumper, leap over the threshold, missing the pistol and landing in the middle of the stage.

All of us can identify with the surreal juxtaposition of images in this hypothetical dream. So much of it is nonsensical. Why should one dream of a telephone connected to a grapevine? Or a pistol partly covered with a frying pan lid? The answer is that this dream has deliberately, logically, methodically re-enacted all of the metaphors used in the initial description of the circumstance faced by this dreamer. He got "wind" of news that came through the communication "grapevine," and he knew that it was going to move him from the "wings to center stage" where he would be obliged to "get into the act." He learned that he was at a "huge threshold." But he was also cautioned to approach from a "different angle." Otherwise, he might "jump the gun;" until then, he'd be wise to "keep a lid on it."

The dream is detailed. It delivers a highly personalized message. And although it communicates in a language that, at first glance, seems perplexing, it is a metaphoric language that we use all the time. It's only that we are unaccustomed to thinking of our speech metaphors being acted out in a literal and cinematic fashion.

This particular dream made use of metaphors that are familiar to us. We have all heard these expressions ever since we learned how to speak, and we use them automatically, usually without being aware that they are visual images representing abstract concepts. Dreams use this category of metaphors all the time.

But dreams also invent metaphors that are not common to our language. By way of illustrating the difference, let's re-examine some metaphors central to a pair of waking dreams already discussed. Austin, while driving his car "hit a wall" and then "broke through the barrier." Those two metaphoric expressions are ones familiar to us. They both refer to the problem of being stymied, and then finding a way to resolve our dilemma.

By contrast, Jeremy had a waking dream in which the central metaphor was an armoire. To him, it symbolized the aggravation of expending excessive energy on a project that didn't warrant it. But there is no common expression that associates furniture with frustration. Ask a dozen people what an armoire means to them, and the responses would probably represent a wide variety of reactions and opinions. In Jeremy's case, the metaphor was one specifically designed to communicate to him.

What this implies is that dream metaphors are personalized. At their deepest level, dreams are a description of the dreamer himself. Certainly, dreams can be about all kinds of things: the past, the future, tragedies, changes, insights, personal triumphs, conflicts, warnings. Some are shocking. Many are confusing. And now and then one can be especially amusing. Name anything in the human condition, and a dream can express it. However, to repeat an observation made in Chapter 6, no matter what type of dream it is, dreams are always about the person who is doing the dreaming. I have never known of an exception to that.

For that reason, when a dream needs to highlight an issue unique to the dreamer, it sometimes is obliged to invent a metaphor, one that will have a meaning that perfectly describes the dreamer's current circumstance. The fact that dreams invent metaphors that we are unfamiliar with complicates our job when we attempt to interpret them. We have to become sleuths, decoders who take an image that seems peculiar, and discover what abstract concept it is intending to represent. It also explains why books that try to offer generic interpretations of dream symbols are of little use. Even dream symbols that are archetypical are filtered through the dreamer's own life experience, and will have vastly different meanings to different people. For example, the symbol of a mother is archetypical in the sense that mothers are those who give us life. But beyond that, if one were to ask ten people to "Tell me about your mother," one would most assuredly get ten unique answers.

While the dream decoding process is work, it is also fun—like doing a crossword puzzle. The five step method gives the process a structure and makes it likely that the dreamer will succeed. And the rewards are enormous. As we have seen from the examples discussed thus far, dreams can be life changing. They offer us invaluable assistance in the form of prompts and reminders, drawing our attention to inconsistencies and conflicts in our thinking. They provide us with warnings, congratulate us when we have done something well, and even offer suggestions in regard to new, more productive life directions.

It can take some practice to attain fluency in dream language, the language of metaphor. As we learned in the hypothetical dream above, the use of metaphor in dreams can become elaborate, even excessive from a literary perspective. But once one has been given an invaluable assist from a dream, one ceases to object to this metaphoric stew. One learns to accept dreams on their own terms, and to take advantage of what they offer us.

We will revisit the subject of dream language in more detail in Chapter 56. For now, as you continue to read, distance yourself from thinking of dream images as being literal. Begin to think metaphorically. The goal, ultimately, is to learn to interpret your own dreams. They will speak to you in metaphors, some of which you will recognize from expressions used in common speech. But many others will be unique inventions of your own subconscious, personalized images brought to your attention to help guide you through life.

PART THREE: WHATEVER YOU PERCEIVE, IS YOU

Part Three explores the radical idea that we participate in the creation of events in our awakened lives, events that logic suggests we have no control over.

11

A woman named Gwen illustrates that when we act on the messages of our waking dreams, our worlds shift around us and our lives change for the better.

Up to this point we have seen examples of odd dream plots at night and peculiar events during the day, all of which have delivered messages to the dreamer suggesting changes he make in his thoughts, attitudes and behavior. This chapter further develops the idea that the choices we make in regard to our thoughts, attitudes and behavior actually influence the nature of our lives. We will specifically address what happens in the dreamer's life when he constructively acts on the dream's message, namely, that the world around him shifts in ways that he could not possibly engineer on his own, especially in regard to waking dreams.

Already we have seen the example of Austin who was obliged to deal with a hair-raising automotive incident, one that seemed to "magically"—if distressingly—manifest in his life. We saw that he was led to examine some attitudes he carried, ones he subsequently changed. As a result, with equal "magic," he was then ushered out of an unsatisfactory work environment and into an ideal one. It has been my observation that the positive outcome he experienced was not a fluke. Rather, it was a logical conclusion in a chain of cause and effect: Austin had a waking dream, responded to the metaphoric message by making an attitude shift, and that led to a happy resolution, including significant changes in aspects of his life that were well beyond his control. I have seen comparable resolutions to waking dreams repeated with impressive consistency over many years.

Now let's examine the waking dream of a young woman named Gwen who was attending a two-day dream workshop I was facilitating. It is one of my favorite waking dreams because the resulting changes that occurred in this dreamer's life were dramatic and immediate and could not possibly have been accomplished by the dreamer on her own. Because the purpose of this chapter is to emphasize what happens in the world around us after we successfully analyze waking dreams, it is not necessary to go through each of the dream interpretation steps in a detailed manner. The reader will recognize them as they come up in the next two paragraphs.

On the first day of the workshop, Gwen asked to work on the following waking dream: She was employed at a restaurant waiting tables during the evening shift, but she was upset to the point of quitting due to continuing confrontations with a male employee who was behaving in a "mean, selfish and nasty" manner—her words. He seemed to take pleasure in causing her distress. During the workshop, I didn't make Gwen's situation any easier when I stressed that all dream symbols are parts of ourselves, and that if she really were interested in resolving her conflict, she needed to take ownership of this obnoxious associate who was appearing in her life as part of an important waking dream. It was a dream that was calling attention to itself so urgently that she could not possibly ignore it.

Her initial reaction was understandable indignation. "I'm not like that! I'm really nice to my colleagues," she insisted. I assured her that I did not doubt her. However, I made the following suggestion: "Tell me about your work." I intentionally left my remark non-directive and vague in case she wanted to consider its meaning in a broader sense—perhaps even metaphorically. She had to think for a moment. Then, to her own surprise, she related that her real work had nothing to do with restaurants. Instead, at the most meaningful level of her life, her work was about experiencing success in regard to personal growth issues she had been struggling with.

Two concepts had now emerged in our dialogue. First, there was the idea of an obnoxious colleague who was being "mean, selfish and nasty." Second, there was the concept that work was about "personal growth." I put the two ideas together. I asked if there was a part of herself that was being "mean, selfish and nasty," causing her distress when she was trying her hardest to facilitate her own "personal growth."

There followed a moment of reflection. This, in turn, was succeeded by a sly smile that said, essentially, "You got me!" Gwen had been struggling with her own ambivalence. Whenever she tried to grow, she was getting in her own way. She was acting as her own "mean, selfish and nasty" agitator, subverting her own efforts at change. She knew how she wanted to be different, but part of her was being an obstructionist, not allowing herself to take the necessary steps. This subversive process that was being acted out inside of herself was subtle, however, and she hadn't really paid enough attention to it. Now that she recognized it, she easily made an attitude shift that allowed for her own progress.

So far our verbal exchange was similar to other conversations one might have where advice is offered in the course of working on personal issues. Using Gwen's obnoxious colleague as a symbol to help her recognize her own self-subverting behavior was a-typical for a counseling session, but otherwise there was nothing unusual about our dialogue. It was what happened afterwards that came as a surprise, for her work environment was about to change dramatically.

I remember suggesting to Gwen that she pay close attention to the atmosphere at the restaurant during her shift that evening. In our discussion she had come to understand that her colleague was a metaphoric representation of her own ambivalence toward personal growth. Now that she had faced her conflict, it was possible that there would be a noticeable change reflecting her new attitude.

The next day all heads turned toward her as she walked back into our conference room. Although there was plenty of expectation all around, no one was more wide-eyed than Gwen herself: "The guy skipped town! His buddy told us that he disappeared. He didn't tell any of his friends, he didn't pay his bills, he didn't give an explanation. He's just gone."

A coincidence? I've witnessed far too many of these events to be seduced by that overly convenient explanation. Gwen's experience followed the same pattern as hundreds of other waking "dreamers." When the dreamer made an attitude shift within himself, his world literally morphed around him. Without Gwen lifting a finger or complaining to her boss or angrily confronting her work associate, the source of her conflict disappeared. Like so many comparable waking dreams that I have been privy to, Gwen's problem ceased to exist after she made the necessary attitude shift within herself.

These kinds of waking-dream happenings vary in their dramatic nature, Gwen's example being especially poignant. Sometimes, they are less cut and dried in their conclusiveness, but they take place far more frequently than most of us are aware of.

A good example of this less-dramatic but conclusive resolution is what happened in regard to Jeremy's waking dream. I had occasion to talk with him a few months after our session. I asked how it had gone when he confronted the owners of the armoire. He had to think for a minute. Then he laughed. "It never came up; the family had a change of mind and took the armoire to someone else." I could tell that Jeremy was uncomfortable even thinking about it. To him the whole episode was simply one of those unpleasant events that life deals us. Further, during our conversation, one could tell that our dream session seemed to him a strange encounter full of implausible ideas, and he couldn't wait to drop the subject. Yet to me, there was indeed a definite cause and effect, a resolution to his problem.

Look closely at the similarities among the sleeping and waking experiences of the various people mentioned thus far: Gwen, while working at her restaurant, shifted something within herself; she changed, and her world then literally transformed itself around her to reflect her new persona. Austin was in the process of resisting his own growth, a conflict which reached a climax symbolically (as well as actually), during an accident in a shopping mall parking lot. He chose to examine the experience metaphorically, focusing on some conflicting messages he was delivering to himself. He altered his unhelpful attitudes, and his employment situation got much better. Anne was made extremely uncomfortable due to guilty feelings after erotic dreams. Once she understood the message, she made an adjustment in her thinking which caused her life to improve significantly. And Jeremy, too, had a partial success. As a result of our discussion, he came to see the relationship between a dream about a mistress and a work project—an armoire—that caused him aggravation. Although he subsequently resisted further dialogue and chose to put our dream interpretation session out of his mind, he and his wife left our meeting with a constructive attitude that was different than the one they arrived with. He would later fail to see any correlation between his change of attitude and the elimination of his problem, but his abrasive situation nevertheless receded from his life without his ever confronting it directly.

All of this suggests that life, rather than being a mysterious—often perplexing, and sometimes distressing—series of random events in which we are inextricably caught, is rather, partly under our own control. The experiences of those above seem to hint that we create these symbols ourselves with our thoughts, attitudes and behaviors, and when we change those characteristics in ourselves, our reality shifts around us. In that sense, it implies that life is less fixed and rigid than we think.

12

Our thoughts, attitudes and behaviors influence the structure of our lives, a concept that is not new.

It is our thoughts, our attitudes and our behaviors that influence the character of our lives and change the nature of our contacts with other people and life situations. It is we who seem to hold the key to changing circumstances that are unacceptable to us, even the ones that seem out of our control. How? By changing ourselves. One of my adages, often repeated during dream workshops, is: Whatever you perceive, is you. I have come to acknowledge this principle in a much more literal, concrete way than is usually accepted in the Western world. I have become firmly convinced that this control we exercise over our own existences goes as far as being capable of influencing our lives in ways that would normally be impossible—not in the sense of performing magic tricks. I am not suggesting that we can wave a wand and manifest anything we consciously desire. The "magic" takes place when we make changes within ourselves. If those changes result in a state of mind that is less-conflicted, then that new-found peace will be reflected in the world around us—in the people we interact with, in the events that happen—in the aspects of our lives over which we appear to have no control.

There are many scholars and thinkers throughout history as well as from our own time who have observed this phenomenon—that our thoughts, attitudes and behaviors influence the nature of our lives in ways that we could not possibly engineer through deliberate, conscious action. In Chapter 4, I related how Fritz Perls was asked, "Is it possible to use an unresolved life situation as if it were a dream and work on it in the same way?" Perls responded, "Yah. Just the same." He knew about this phenomenon. He saw the connection between an individual's inner self and his outer world. Since he was working primarily with people and their emotional distress, he tended to view this as a tool to be used specifically in therapy. Would he have agreed with me, in a more general sense, that a healthy, aware person can actually make the cast of characters change, the plot veer off in a new direction, the outcome shift from unsatisfactory to fulfilling? From all I have learned about him, I believe he would have.

Carl Jung knew about this connection between our psyches and the world that manifests around us. His book, *Synchronicity—An A-causal Connecting Principle*, is devoted largely to the idea that there is an invisible, subtle bond between our inner states of mind and the outer world. Teacher and philosopher, Joseph Campbell, understood the connection as well. One of the principal themes of his lectures and writings is as follows: Stop for a moment, and look at who you are at the deepest level. What motivates you? What inspires you? What makes you want to get up in the morning and face the world on fire with your own enthusiasm? Arrange your life to live it in such a way that you are constantly nurturing those qualities. If you do, you will find that there is a kind of magic that takes place. You will see that the world begins to actively cooperate with you and help you in ways that you could not possibly have arranged for by yourself; you could not have engineered this degree of collaboration.

Campbell was fond of saying that our constructive inner changes cause “doors [to] open where there were only walls."[8] It is my contention that one of the best ways to find these "doors" in our lives is to work with dreams, both waking and sleeping.

As related earlier, Shakespeare wrote about this phenomenon. Native Americans also consider it in their intimate association with the earth and animals. And cultures other than our Euro-centric Western one have taken the concept much further than we have. The Chinese, for example, have gone so far as to make an art form out of it, only they approach it in reverse. The practice of feng shui is based on the acknowledgment that our surroundings and our sense of self are inextricably linked.[9] The Chinese approach is to adjust the environment in such a way that it brings peace of mind and beneficial results to the individuals inhabiting it. At first reading this doesn’t seem unusual. Western architects, for example, do the same thing with their designs, using shape and space and proximity. In addition, Western Europeans and Americans have discovered that violence in prisons and schools can be significantly lessened by something as simple as the careful choosing of paint colors on walls.[10] Yet the Chinese practice of feng shui goes much further than the recognition that environment can have an effect on one’s mood and sense of well-

---

[8] www.brainyquotes.com/quotes/authors/j/joseph_campbell.html

[9] Collins, Terah Kathryn; The Western Guide to Feng Shui; pp. 1-3.

[10] http://psychology.about.com/od/sensationandperception.a/color_pink.html

being. Practitioners of this art form claim to be able to adjust an environment in such a way as to increase wealth, strengthen marriage ties, promote health and add to longevity. To them, the connection between a person's environment and attitude is inseparable.

I, too, have found that the link between objective life and our attitudes about the world goes far beyond what we tend to accept in general. We will continue to explore that link, delving more deeply into other examples, as we consider the possibility that our world—with everything in it—shifts around us when we change our thoughts, attitudes and behaviors.

PART FOUR: YOU HAVE TO OWN IT

Using the distressing experience of a woman named Ellen as an example, Part Four examines the need to take responsibility for creating the unpleasant aspects of our lives. This includes those aspects over which we think we have no control.

13

A woman named Ellen attends dream classes and asks for help with a waking dream.

Groups are excellent settings for dream work. There is something about this dynamic—ten or twelve enthusiasts reflecting ideas off each other in a constructive dialogue—that leads to particularly meaningful insights. Invariably someone has a perspective that no one else (including me) considered, and the exploration often goes deeper, reaching more profound levels than when a dreamer tries to work alone. Knowing that you're among sympathetic fellow dreamers, one feels a sense of support and trust that helps break down barriers. It is my favorite way to work with people and their dreams, especially when the dreams become challenging to the person having them.

It was in exactly this kind of setting that a delightful woman named Ellen made an important—if initially painful—discovery about the changeable nature of life and her own role in manifesting the "bad" things that were coming her way. Ellen was a middle-aged mother-of-three with a sunny disposition, one that even managed to shine through the clouds of contentious and draining divorce proceedings that had been eating away at her energy and self-respect for well over a year. She had initially joined the class as a way to escape, mentally, from her woes—to do something "fun." Certainly the class had started out as a diversion for her. Dreams are peculiar at best, and their strangeness can be entertaining. Watching the struggles and insights of others helped take her thoughts away from herself; it was therapeutic.

Through the first several weeks Ellen maintained a razor wit, and often had the class laughing uproariously. Predictably, the butt of her humor tended to be her estranged husband and his unreasonableness. They were an affluent couple, and there were plenty of resources to use against each other in the psychological torment that seems to accompany many separations. He was apparently doing his best to make her life miserable, and she was determined to prove that she had no intention of being intimidated. The rivalry continued to intensify, but when it finally focused on the welfare of their children, her mood noticeably shifted. As far as she was concerned, the contest had now evolved into something beyond sport; frankly, she was alarmed. "I just want it all to stop," she confessed during one evening class. The group became subdued in its sympathy for her. One classmate held her hand, and others were lost in their own memories of comparable personal wars. Through it all there was a palpable outpouring of concern which made my own reaction to her announcement seem callous.

David: How badly do you want it to stop, Ellen?

Ellen: I beg your pardon?

David: I mean, are you content with this evening's show of sympathy from your friends here, or do you really want it over? Because, if you do, it's going to take some serious work on your part.

Ellen, startled by my comments, retreated into a pensive shell and didn't respond. After an awkward silence, I finally guided the group discussion in other directions—although it never recovered its usual spontaneity. Nor did Ellen return for the next three or four sessions. The group, though still enthusiastic, felt her absence, and possibly wondered at the wisdom of my approach. But about a month after her departure, Ellen reappeared. If anything, she looked more haggard than before. In those few weeks she seemed to have aged, and one got the impression that she was perpetually on the verge of crying. "If you think you can help," she announced to me, "I'll try anything at this point." After some warm hugs all around and expressions of pleasure at her return, the group settled down, and she became the focus of the meeting. Because of the urgency of Ellen's issues, the class initially played a quieter part in the dialogue, preferring to let me guide. Nevertheless, their supportive presence was vital, and they would eventually come roaring back into prominence after Ellen worked her way to more solid ground.

David: Well, Ellen, you've been coming to these classes long enough to know what the approach is. [Pause] I think you even know what I'm going to tell you.

Ellen: I'm dreading what you're going to say.

David: Don't worry! We'll all be here for help and support. The fact is, you've seen the principles at work over and over. The only difference is that, up to now, the incidents we've discussed have been relatively minor. They've caused some annoyance, sometimes some laughter, or a little stinging, but nothing bigger. This one, though, is going to take more of an overhaul on your part, and I make no promises that it's going to be easy. [Ellen sighs audibly.] Why don't we start by reviewing some of the basics, and we'll work up to it gradually. OK?

14

Ellen reflects on the dream-related concepts of projection, personal ownership and change.

During the months that Ellen had been a regular member of our dream class, she had been a lively, popular participant. Mostly, she was an observer of the waking and sleeping dreams of others in the class. When she finally felt comfortable enough to ask formally for help with her marital conflict—a struggle she understood intellectually as being a waking dream—she balked. The idea of having to put in the necessary amount of work to make changes in her life seemed overwhelming. She was suddenly faced with the prospect of having to take to heart the unorthodox principles she had heard discussed so often. But when she returned to class after an absence of a few weeks, it was with a new determination and an even stronger desire to see the process through.

When I resumed working with Ellen, I began by reviewing the psychological term "projection." There were similarities between the concept of projection and what I was going to be asking of her when we began working on her waking dream symbols. But there were also important differences which needed to be clarified.

She knew from our classes that projection is the act of attributing one's own attitude, feeling or idea to someone else. A projection can involve any kind of thought—happy or distressed—but in counseling sessions, often the projection is a negative attitude. Put in the crudest terms, this type of projection is a form of blaming, especially if it involves a personal issue that is uncomfortable—like a sense of guilt or vehement dislike. Our image of ourselves does not easily encompass these kinds of objectionable thoughts, so we try to convince ourselves that they're really not coming from us, but rather, from "that guy over there." There is an aspect of denial to them; we don't take credit for our own unsavory opinions.

Children do this rather transparently. ("Mary's being mean to me," says Johnny when, in fact, it's Johnny who's just thwacked Mary and made her cry.) We adults become more subtle about it, but it's still the same game. ("I don't like Susan because she's so disapproving of others.") We all do this from time to time, and one of the goals of a counseling session can be to lead an individual away from this unproductive behavior. The person can then be more aware of what motivates his reactions to the things in his life that are unpleasant. It's a way of taking responsibility: "It's true that I don't like Susan's tendency to disapprove of others, but if I look closely at myself, I see that I can be just as critical. Maybe I should pay more attention to my own disapproving nature." Dealing with projection and realizing that we often exhibit the same distasteful behaviors we observe in others, is an important, healthy thing to do.

Ellen was not projecting, however. She was well aware of her caustic attitude toward her husband. At first, she had even prided herself in her ability to jab back at him when he was verbally assaulting her. She took responsibility for her attitude and behaviors.

Nevertheless, I was now going to demand of Ellen a degree of ownership of the conflict between her husband and herself that represented a gigantic leap beyond the concept of projection. She was embroiled in a real-life legal battle in which her estranged husband was acting like a boor and doing his best to make her existence a living nightmare. In the midst of this hell, I was now audaciously—certainly controversially—going to suggest that the reason he was behaving this way toward her was because, at a subliminal level, she created his despicable behavior herself. I was going to argue that there was little or no difference between this true-life divorce trauma and a literal nightmare. In a process nearly identical to that of a sleeping dream, I suggested that her subconscious had created waking-dream symbols, using her husband to express metaphorically her own internal conflict, an internal conflict that had nothing to do with her divorce. Her subconscious was alerting her to this conflict while she was wide awake. Indeed, this subliminal activity had reached a feverish pitch, and as with Austin and his cruise control, it was now threatening her physical and emotional well-being. It was my goal to help Ellen uncover the source of her inner discord.

Before we embarked on the use of the 5 Steps of dream interpretation, it was important for her to understand that change was inevitable and to examine some possible outcomes to her ordeal. For instance, she could win this battle against her husband, in which case she would undoubtedly come away feeling victorious—if exhausted—but she would certainly become different in the process.

Or, she could lose the fight and feel depressed and demoralized. That, too, would represent a change. However, both of those scenarios involved combat with her husband, something she now wanted to avoid. For that reason, I suggested a third possibility—that she focus her attention exclusively on making changes within herself rather than engaging her husband in a war of manipulation. If she deliberately worked on changing her attitudes and expectations, perhaps the outer conflict would be modified as well—modified beyond anything she could personally engineer. What did she have to lose?

Ellen had reached a state of desperation. She agreed with me that some kind of change was inevitable, so courageously, she decided to see what positive results might come from this different approach.

To begin with, I reminded her that she was in the middle of a dream—a waking dream—and that her job was to work with and learn from the symbols. Over time we would go through all five steps of the dream interpretation technique. She had already related her dilemma to the class (Step 1). Next, I would help her isolate the symbols (Step 2), and then we would work together to complete the rest of the steps. I warned her that, when we got to Step 4, it would involve owning the metaphors, actually taking responsibility for creating the abhorrent behaviors of her estranged husband. This would be difficult. I would be asking her to accept an idea that was well beyond the concept of projection. I would be insisting that she consider the radical idea that, at an unconscious level, she herself, like a playwright, had written the script of her husband's abusiveness. I would certainly help her through this unusual approach, but ultimately, it was up to her to take the initiative.

In the next several chapters, we will follow Ellen as she bravely accepts the challenge and goes through the demanding—sometimes overwhelming—process of seeing her waking dream through to the profound understanding it brings to her at the end.

15

Ellen works her way through Step 3 of the interpretation process, the "Tell me about it!" part.

Over the weeks that Ellen had been attending our dream class, we had all become familiar with her circumstance and the symbols related to her predicament. For that reason, on the evening that I began to work with her, we were able to skip the first two steps of dream interpretation: Relate the dream and Isolate the symbols. We went directly to Step 3: Interpret the symbols as metaphors, the "Tell me about it!" part.

David: Tell me about husbands.

Ellen: You mean mine?

David: No, not yet. Let's start a bit more generally than that. Just tell me about husbands as a concept.

Ellen: Well, they're supposed to be partners. They're supposed to be your friend. They're supposed to be supportive and helpful. [pause] I guess there actually are some husbands out there who stand up for you when things get tough. But I sure as hell don't have one. [Ellen's tears begin to fall.]

David: Anything else you want to say about husbands in general?

Ellen: [sighs] I guess in traditional families the husband is the breadwinner, the one who goes out and gets a job, goes out and works. It was that way in our house until all of this exploded in my face.

David: Good! Now tell me about your husband.

Ellen: Oh, Christ! [sigh] What's not to say? He's deceitful. He's conniving. He's dishonest. He lies. He's malicious. He's backbiting. He's sneaky. He's vindictive. [pause] Is that enough yet? Oh yeah, and he's shitty in bed. [uncomfortable group laughter]

David: Tell me about divorce.

Ellen: It's when you've finally had enough. When you can't stand it anymore, and you want out.

David: Tell me about the legal proceedings of divorce.

Ellen: God! That's a war. Like to the bitter end. It's like sticking two insane fighters in a small room and watching while one kills the other.

David: Tell me about your children.

Ellen: [a long, long pause, then, through tears] They're the most precious part of my life. In some ways they are my life. They literally came from me, from my body, from my being. And I'm supposed to be protecting them. But how can I with all this crap going on?

David: OK. Nicely done, Ellen. Sometimes this kind of raw, candid sharing can be difficult, but you did well.

Ellen: [Pointing at me and reacting to my prior assertion that she would be obliged to "own" her symbols] David, I'm telling you I'm not like him. I don't do those things to people. I don't take some kind of sadistic pleasure in ruining lives.

David: I know that. But actually, you don't have to worry about what I may think, because my attitudes about you don't make any difference. As you've seen plenty of times in here, when I tell your dream back to you, I'm going to do my best to stay as far out of it as I can. If I do it right, the symbols will tell the story. They can do that more accurately than either one of us trying to figure it out on our own. [To the class] So. Why don't we all take a short break. When we come back we'll let those symbols have their say.

16

Dream symbols sometimes can frighten, shock, and offend us.

Presenting Ellen's story has a twofold purpose. First, it represents an excellent example of a courageous individual using the waking dream phenomenon to wage a battle successfully against huge issues in her life. Second, in telling Ellen's story, certain characteristics of dreams will need to be clarified. For that reason, in this chapter we will take a detour to explain these principles; we will take a close look at the sometimes-unseemly nature of dream symbols.

Ellen's symbols were going to help her tell a story about herself, a story that would bring insight and assist her in resolving her dilemma. When that happened, the symbols would recede from her life. In the meantime, they were overwhelming and frightening.

During dream classes, many symbols seem ludicrous at first. There is consistent delight and amusement in sorting through the absurdity to find a gem hidden in its midst. But occasionally, as we've seen with Ellen, dreams can be scary—their symbols looming over us in foreboding, threatening fashion.

It is in these instances that we are most inclined to deny our involvement in creating them. Ellen's emphatic, "I'm not like him," expressed an unwillingness to identify with something in her life that was appalling to her. Her reaction was nearly identical to the one Anne experienced in Chapter 8, when as a happily married woman, she was repeatedly having dreams of illicit romantic encounters. How can such alien thoughts and situations be a part of our thinking if we find them unsavory?

The answer is that dream symbols have a complete disregard for our sense of decorum. They simply don't care whether or not we are confused by them, repulsed by them, shocked by them, or terrified of them. In fact, since their first need is to be remembered, they often come to our attention precisely because we are appalled by their seemingly uninvited appearance into our thoughts. A friend of mine, in a sleeping dream, once watched himself use a pistol to shoot his father in the back of the head at point blank range. He was so horrified by his memory of this image that it took him several days to get past its emotional impact enough to begin working on the symbol. When he finally did, it turned out to be constructive—a "coming of age" dream about finally, belatedly putting an end to some old "parental" messages he had been giving himself for years. This was certainly a good example of a symbol that was oblivious to his sensibilities. And he has never forgotten the dream!

I try to encourage dreamers to get used to this aspect of dreaming because, not only are such symbols important, but often, they are amusing if one can get past attitudes about what is or isn't appropriate. One of the most famous examples of this comes from Carl Jung. When he was a young boy, Jung found himself struggling with an inner conflict between the narrow orthodoxy of his local church—of which his own father was the minister—and his need to explore spirituality beyond the tenets of his strict religious upbringing. As his conflict grew, he began, vaguely, to be aware of a symbolic image that wanted to make its way, front and center, into his thoughts—an image that he could sense would be socially and religiously blasphemous. Even though he was just a youngster, he did manage, for days, to struggle successfully against his urge to acknowledge its presence. But finally he knew he was going to have to give in to it, however awful the vision might be.

I gathered all my courage, as though I were about to leap forthwith into hell-fire, and let the thought come. I saw before me the cathedral [and] the blue sky. God sits on His golden throne, high above the world—and from under the throne an enormous turd falls upon the sparkling new roof, shatters it, and breaks the walls of the cathedral asunder.[11]

With this symbol came an understanding of profound importance to Jung. The idea that God might have disdain for the church by defecating on it, helped him clearly delineate the difference between orthodoxy and personal spiritual exploration, and it would be central to his approach to life and work ever after. Nevertheless, one can certainly appreciate a young, religiously conscientious boy's distress as he tried desperately to avoid allowing such a taboo image into his

---

[11] Jung, Carl; Memories, Dreams, Reflections; p. 39.

awareness. It was only much later, when Jung was an adult, that he would see the humor in it.

No matter how symbols appear to us—bowel movements, horrifying pictures of fathers shot in the head, implausible events with malfunctioning cruise controls, or the conflicts of marital warfare—they force their way into our awareness so that we can't help but pay attention to them. That is their purpose, and that was what Ellen was about to confront as she began to see her own symbols in a new light.

17

Ellen's dream is repeated back to her: Step 4: Retell the dream, using and owning the metaphors.

The symbols of a sleeping dream can always be attributed to an invention of imagination, but Ellen was facing "real life" symbols. The stakes seemed high in her case, and it was going to be painful for her to confront Step 4 of the dream interpretation technique: Retell the dream using and owning the metaphors. I began by organizing her symbols into a story:

David: Ellen, if this dream were mine, I'd say that there is a part of me that is supposed to be my partner, my friend. It's supposed to be supportive and helpful. This part of me is supposed to stand up for me when things get tough. Traditionally, it's the part of me that is the breadwinner, meaning that it's the part of me that would normally have some sort of job designed to help and support me. But instead, this part of me is being deceitful, conniving, dishonest, lying, malicious, sneaky, vindictive—and, to continue using your own words, "shitty in bed." Ellen, I'm guessing that what you are saying, metaphorically, in this last remark, is that this part of me "doesn't love me very skillfully."

I'm sick of being associated with this part of me, to the point where I've finally had enough. I can't stand it anymore and I want out. So I'm engaged in a war with myself. And it's like watching two insane fighters in a small room; I'm watching while one part of me kills the other part of me. And the worst of it is that there's a third part of me—really the most precious part of my life, a part of me that came from my body—from my being—that I'm supposed to be nurturing and protecting. But how can I, with all this crap going on?

By now Ellen's crying was unrestrained. We waited quietly until it subsided. There were some jokes about needing to buy stock in a tissue company, some gentle laughter, some hands on her shoulders, and when she was calm again, I started talking to her once more.

David: Ellen, if this dream were mine, I'd wonder if there was a conflict going on inside of myself in which the part of me that is supposed to be supportive has turned against me. I would ask myself if this conflict was interfering with my nurturing of "the most precious thing in my life." I think you said this precious thing came from your body; it's something that you're supposed to be protecting, but can't with "all this crap going on." Can you help me understand? Is there anything in your life that seems to relate to this description?

18

Ellen tells the story of a traumatic occurrence in her life when she was 16-years-old.

At the end of the last chapter, I asked Ellen if she could see any correlation between the metaphorical interpretation I offered regarding her waking dream and current circumstances in her world. This question signaled the beginning of our work on Step 5: Explore the dream's relevance in your life.

Normally during a dream class, I would ask a dreamer to examine recent events in his life for clues to the dream's message. But in Ellen's case, the waking dream symbols were so intense and frightening that I was not surprised when she responded by telling us the following story from her teenage years.

Ellen related that, as a small girl growing up in a largely agrarian town in central Michigan, she had become obsessed with ballet. She began taking lessons, and at first, no one thought much about it because it was one of those things that so many little girls do. The difference was that Ellen had an ideal dancer's physique. She also had grace, an excellent sense of rhythm, showmanship and the innate drive to put in the necessary hours and concentration. Her teacher recognized her promise, and after the first few years, recommended that she continue her study at a highly respected dance studio in Detroit. The commute was long involving several afternoons a week. Her family, sympathetic to her commitment, finally moved their entire household to be closer. Her father even changed his job.

As Ellen's ballet skills progressed, she drew more and more attention to herself until, at age 16, she was singled out for a prominent role in the city's annual production of *The Nutcracker* ballet. This attracted a good deal of media attention including a series of news stories, and it was capped by a write-up in the Sunday arts section—complete with a large photo—touting her as the new, up-and-coming local star. Though still a teen, she would be dancing as part of a professional troop and would be accompanied by a full symphony orchestra. She learned that a good percentage of her extended family was traveling to Detroit, as was her first dance teacher and several of her friends from those early days. Some of these people would be coming considerable distances, attending the opening night performance along with about 2,500 other audience members.

The pressure began to mount, but she was not overly concerned. She'd already had plenty of experience dancing in front of people, and she'd built up lots of confidence. Yet, something was different this time. Perhaps it was the extent of the scrutiny she was under; a critic would be in the audience. Also, she had never danced in such a grand venue. On the day she told us this story, decades after the event, she still couldn't pinpoint exactly what happened. But shortly before that first performance, she was so overwhelmed by stage fright that she almost had to be pushed in front of the curtain when her cue came.

Her performance was a disaster from the first moment. Her body seemed to have forgotten everything it had learned over those many years. She trembled uncontrollably. She forgot her steps, ran into other dancers, and at one point, fell. She has no memory of how she made it to the end of her scene. For her, it was a nightmare.

Ellen told us that the pain and subsequent anguish she felt were even beyond tears. It was as if she went into shock. To make matters infinitely worse, the newspaper critic—the same journalist who had interviewed her for her Sunday article—chose to be particularly virulent in his review. He cast aspersions on her ability as a dancer, he lambasted her for her lack of intelligence, and he even caustically implied that her teachers were incompetent for not recognizing her mediocrity. This would have been a hard pill for anyone to swallow, but for a 16-year-old it was devastating.

Her degradation was spectacular and complete. A substitute was called in to do the rest of her performances. She found that she couldn't face school or her friends or even her family. She withdrew, became antisocial with her peers, and she never put ballet slippers on her feet again.

19

Ellen struggles to understand the relevance of her complex waking dream.

As painful as it was for Ellen to relive her memories of her dance fiasco, her experience of expressing them to us that evening was the beginning of profound changes she made over the next weeks and months, changes that did not come easily at first. These transformations, like those made by other dreamers introduced earlier, would eventually result in actual shifts in her physical reality. The circumstances of her life would be altered, bringing changes that would be difficult to explain outside the realm of the waking dream.

Ellen had a long struggle to endure before those kinds of changes would take place. For her, there was an added complication, namely having to reach far into her past to find the source of her conflict. As we have seen with Austin and his cruise control and Gwen with her obnoxious restaurant colleague, a series of waking dream symbols usually highlights an issue that is current in the dreamer's life.

Yet when I asked Ellen to explore her divorce symbols as something relevant to her, she spontaneously reached back a quarter of a century to an incident that occurred when she was a teenager. Not only did this hint at the length of time these conflicts had been plaguing her, but it suggested that she would need to examine the counterproductive behavior pattern of many past years to see how it still affected her in the present moment. She would need to consider changing behaviors that had become deep-seeded and habitual. Finally, she would need to make the metaphoric connection between those destructive behaviors being played out within herself and her husband's outward maliciousness toward her.

This was a tall order complicated further by the fact that the divorce proceedings themselves were so all-consuming. In the beginning she had difficulty seeing a connection between her personal behavior and her outer circumstances; she saw no link between her dream symbols and the way she lived. More than once she almost gave up. She would become distracted from her dream work by yet another legal squabble, and the momentum she had built up would be lost. It was exhausting for her, and there were always the children to be mindful of and to be worried about.

Yet Ellen did make the changes, and those changes resulted in her living in an altered world afterwards.

20

Ellen begins to understand the connection between her dream symbols and the way she was living her life.

Ellen's growth happened in fits and starts. First, she came to understand that significant parts of her personality were a façade. Much of the sunny disposition and the biting humor were masks she used to hold people—including herself—at bay, so she wouldn't have to face her own inner turmoil. It was a revelatory evening when she saw the connection between this behavior and her dream symbols. All those words she used to lambaste her estranged husband—words like deceitful, conniving, dishonest, sneaky, lying—suddenly rang a loud bell within herself. These words described exactly what she was doing when she played her mental games to divert attention away from what was painful.

Next, she came to see how the rest of those adjectives—the more caustic ones like malicious, backbiting and vindictive—were relevant as well. She had been feeling anger for a long time, anger at the unfairness of life. Part of her game-playing was an expression of this rage. She was surprised at the extent to which her dream symbols really were a description of herself.

The irony was that it had been exactly that seething side of her persona that had been the key to her evolving beyond the initial depression which followed her dance fiasco. Everything she had eventually succeeded in doing in her life—getting through college, marrying into affluent circumstances, becoming a respected and well-liked personality in her various social circles—was due to her ability to bypass her pain and "tough" her way into a new existence. That represented a large part of what was so difficult for her. It seemed that when she had been true to herself, dancing her heart out, she had failed. By contrast, when she had created a mask and lived her life using the crutch of her façade, she had succeeded, at least better than she ever had before in her life. Now it seemed that the message being delivered by her intense waking dream involving her divorce, was that she give up the mask entirely. This was a scary proposition, and she was, indeed, engaged in an inner war that was like two insane fighters in a small room punching it out to the death. How could she trust what was real when it had let her down so miserably in the past?

21

Ellen is helped by a particularly poignant dream symbol.

As Ellen dissected the many symbols in her complex waking dream, she came to understand that she had been living a life that was, in large part, a façade, one she had erected around herself for emotional protection. For her, the prospect of letting it go was frightening, and she wondered how she might accomplish that.

She found the answer to her question when she examined another part of her dream, the section about "the most precious part" of her that she was supposed to be protecting. Other symbols in her dream were more dramatic and had drawn her attention to themselves right away. It was only later that she took a closer look at this symbol and realized how poignant it was.

This symbol had seemed clear at first. "The precious part" had "come from her body; from her being." She had been a dancer, and that made perfect sense. But it had been years since she had danced. Half her life had intervened without assistance from leotards and tights. How could this symbol still be relevant?

I reminded her of still another of the symbols in her complex waking dream, the one about the husband who is the breadwinner and has the job. If her "job" when she was a teenager was to dance, what did she think her current job entailed? She responded that she was a live-at-home mom, so she really didn't have any actual employment, except that she was raising her kids. I pointed out to her that, in her own words, she had described her kids as coming from her body, from her being.

David: Ellen, if this dream were mine I'd ask myself if, rather than protecting my children, I was, in some way, poisoning them with deceit. After all, every day the part of me that has the "job" of raising them is getting up and greeting them with a façade, a mask. I am presenting them with a role model that is motivated by anger and malicious backbiting. I'm supposed

> to be protecting them, "but how can I with all this crap going on?"

Clarifying that particular section of the dream was, apparently, the missing link in Ellen's overall understanding of her experience. It represented the turning point in her healing process. After hearing her parenting behavior dissected in this fashion—dissected using her own dream symbols—she grew silent for a notable length of time. When she emerged from her pensiveness it seemed that she had faced something inside herself and had come to a decision. Before that moment, had anyone in the class been asked if they thought Ellen was disciplined and focused, they would have said yes, unquestionably. But the Ellen who emerged from her brief meditation seemed like a new being. One could see on her face and in her eyes that "the fight to the death in the small room" was about to reach its climax. No one had the slightest doubt about which of the Ellens was going to prevail. Watching her change in this fashion was like cheering for a favorite sports team on the verge of a spectacular victory. It was exhilarating even for those of us who were spectators.

22

Another of Ellen's important dream symbols is revealed.

Ellen had come a long way. She had bridged an important gap by acknowledging that her current style of living was a direct result of her teenage trauma. She saw that her dance fiasco had instilled defensive behavior patterns that helped her through her initial depression but were counterproductive in the long run. She was startled to recognize that the metaphoric descriptions she gave of her husband's abusiveness accurately described herself. This understanding was vital to her healing process. According to the tenets of waking dream behavior, the key to altering her husband's aggressive unfairness was to make changes within herself. If the actions he was taking against her were a metaphoric reflection of her state of mind, then the way to change this interaction was to shift her own attitude and approach to life.

But Ellen had not dealt with every symbol in her lengthy dream. We had yet to discuss the symbol of her children. Dealing with them symbolically was important, not only because of the further insight it would bring her, but because it was an opportunity for her to learn that not all dream symbols are uncomfortable. I assured her that, unlike the horse pills she had been obliged to swallow until now, dealing with the symbol of her children was going to be more like savoring a dessert.

It was obvious that Ellen's new determination was motivated by her deep love and affection for her three youngsters—a pre-teen girl, an eight-year-old boy and another girl, a first grader. That love, in itself, represented the noblest of qualities in the human spirit, and nothing else really mattered. But taken from the perspective of the waking dream, her children—like her husband—represented a metaphoric dynamic working inside herself. The difference was that, whereas her husband symbolized a huge—often overwhelming—conflict she was attempting to resolve, her children were part of something "precious" that she was helping to "raise" and nurture, again inside herself. What was this precious thing? I wanted to explore that question with her. Whatever it was, she could rest assured that it was something as beautiful and as wondrous as she found her growing children to be; if this precious thing were not growing within, it would not be reflected metaphorically in the waking dream symbols of her outer life. It was as simple as that. If she could keep this in mind as she struggled to make the mammoth shift from the "old" masked Ellen to the "new" more open, less angry one, it could help motivate her as she worked her way toward a healthier perspective on her life.

By now Ellen was well versed in the five dream interpretation steps and our exchange was smooth:

David: Ellen, tell me about children.

Ellen: [thoughtful at first] They're young humans. They're not mature yet. They're innocent. They're not jaded or bogged down by complications. They come bursting into a room, and they may be loud and annoying, but they're so light—so optimistic. They make me envious; I want to be like them.

There was a pause. Then:

David: Ellen, if this dream were mine, I'd say that there is a part of me living inside of myself that is populated by young humans. This part of me isn't mature yet. It's innocent. It's not jaded or bogged down by complications. At times it may be loud and annoying, but it's so light, so optimistic. This part of me makes me envious. I want to be like it.

Ellen became extremely quiet. Analyzing "children" as a dream symbol was a new piece of the puzzle for her, the first one that gave her hope. In her own words, children represented parts of herself that were "young," and not "bogged down by complications." Most importantly, they were "optimistic." One could see her trying this aspect of herself on for size like an attractive piece of clothing. If there was something young and optimistic growing within her, then there was reason to look forward to the future. As the weeks went by, she used the "children" symbol to anchor herself and give herself strength when life became overwhelming. She had no trouble identifying with it; she knew it was growing inside of her, knew it was what was driving her to succeed, knew it would become an increasingly dominant part of her persona the healthier she became. Now, for the first time, she could identify with it, put a label on it, rely on it to urge her forward.

In the midst of hell, this optimism was a beacon. Because she could use it to guide her, she finally had a clearer understanding of the issues that weighed so heavily on her. For the first time she saw her divorce as the secondary phenomenon in her life. The primary one, she now realized, was the equally tumultuous change going on in her own psyche. Yes, it necessitated the painful destruction of a false front, but she now realized that what awaited her after her transformation was much healthier. That understanding alone represented an enormous shift on her part.

23

Ellen begins to explore the possibility that there is a relationship between her dreams and the events of her "outer" world.

Ellen had started to consider the possibility that the turmoil she was experiencing with her estranged husband wasn't really the cause of her distress, but was, rather, a symptom of another crisis being acted out within herself. We had already worked to dissect the waking dream of her legal battles. In doing so, she had come to recognize that she tended to approach life from a state of anger, facing it daily through a mask, a personality façade. All of this was enlightening to her, but none of it seemed to motivate her forcefully enough to make changes until she realized that her children, for whom she was the primary adult influence, were suffering as a result of her own inner warfare. Her growing family was being subjected to a front of superficial humor and lightness that actually masked powerful discontent. That understanding was a revelation for her, and one could almost watch the shifts begin to take place within her as she took the first steps toward embracing healthier attitudes. These changes began with her new awareness of her counterproductive approach to life. That, in turn, led to a more conscientious effort to recognize her detrimental attitudes. Now, whenever she saw them in herself, she would make note of them and bring them to class for discussion.

Once again, an important thesis of this book is that when changes are occurring inside a dreamer, then that person will begin to notice comparable shifts in his physical reality. Those of us in Ellen's dream class were certainly curious to see if any changes occurred, and we were anxious to stay in touch with her growth process.

The first opportunity occurred during class a week after her initial breakthrough. When asked if she had noticed anything different in the difficult relationship she had with her husband and his legal team, Ellen told us that it hadn't been a good week to make those kinds of observations.

David: How so?

Ellen: Well, the lawyers were in court on another case, so I couldn't tell if they were going to hassle me or not.

This announcement resulted in some snickering. Ellen looked around, confused, not understanding what she had said that was so amusing. She was soon enlightened by her cohorts (who, for the sake of simplicity, will be identified by letters of the alphabet).

AA: Ellen, did you get hassled by lawyers this week?

Ellen: No.

AA: Did you get hassled the week before?

Ellen: Yeah. But they were busy this week. I mean, that's not a change from what's been going on. This has all happened before.

BB: But you did have an easier week?

Ellen: Yeah. But, like I said, it doesn't mean anything. If you really want to know, I spent most of the week dreading phone calls, so I didn't exactly relax.

David: OK. So this week could have been a coincidental blip.

Ellen: Sure. Next week they'll probably go right back to how they've been all along.

David: But if, instead of that happening, you keep having more weeks like this last one, would that begin to suggest a trend?

Ellen: Oh God, would I love that!

24

Ellen's mindset is responsible for her rejection of clues that suggest her new attitudes are constructively influencing her life.

Were the outer events in Ellen's life a result of her new understanding, accompanied by the new attitudes that she was carefully nurturing, or was this a coincidence with more grief to come? She would be delighted if it were a positive trend, but there was too little evidence to reach conclusions. Only time would tell if the shifts the class commented on were consequential.

Significant to note is that, rather than staying in neutral and simply collecting the data of her daily experiences, she automatically rejected the idea that her new attitudes might have influenced her outward circumstances. She dismissed the possibility that there was a connection between her new realizations and the previous week's relative lack of interference from her estranged husband's attorneys. She seemed to be expecting some kind of obvious sign rather than simply observing the subtler patterns of her daily experiences. This kind of disregard is, unfortunately, something we all have experienced from time to time. As a result, we can miss important clues as they come along. When we look for these kinds of shifts in our lives, we sometimes expect some sort of cosmic fireworks display. We become so fixated on what we think the solution ought to be that we miss an alternative way out of our dilemma when it presents itself: I'm having financial difficulties so, obviously, I need to win the lottery. I don't like my house so, obviously, I need to move. I'm not getting any dates with men so, obviously, I need a new wardrobe. While any of those remedies might work, they will not necessarily solve the problem, and there are untold numbers of possible alternative solutions.

Until she was questioned by her classmates, Ellen had begun to create just such a mind-set, an expectation that, if the waking dream were valid, she would know it by a certain response she was looking for from her husband's attorneys. The fact that her life might have begun to steer itself in a slightly different direction, leaving her relatively free of contentious interactions for a week, was a circumstance she not only ignored but actively dismissed.

25

Ellen finally sees a clear connection between the symbols of her ongoing waking dream and the unpleasant events in her daily life.

Ellen's next few weeks were not easy ones. The behavior of her husband and his attorneys was erratic. Sometimes these adversaries caused her grief and significant annoyance. At other times they seemed to ignore her entirely. At first she could see no consistency, no connection between their mercurial performance and herself. But every time she had a bad week, her classmates would gently ask if, perhaps, she had slipped back into old habits. This was hard going. No one likes to feel victimized only to be told by friends that she is an active participant in the process—indeed, the primary instigator. There was understandable resistance on her part. There were tears. There was plenty of her acerbic wit. At one point it even seemed as if she might quit. To her immense credit, she never gave up.

Finally, after a period of several weeks, she began to see what she thought might be a connection between the attitudes that had motivated her during a given time span and the resulting behavior of her husband and his lawyers.

No one grows in a straight line. In order to alter her caustic approach to life, she was going to have to break habits that were not only entrenched, but were ones she had come to associate with her survival. This was a mammoth undertaking, and it was inevitable that her progress would include a certain number of setbacks. Finally there came an evening that I doubt anyone in the class will ever forget.

CC: [to Ellen] You look a little scrawny tonight. You OK?

Ellen: I'm fine. [Pause]

BB: You sure about that? You don't look so good.

Ellen: I've got something I want to say. It's just a little hard, that's all.

David: Take your time, Ellen.

Ellen: It's about my Ex. [collective groan]

CC: Uh-oh! Is he at it again?

Ellen: Kind of. But not really. Or maybe yes, but sort of both at once. [Laughter]

David: You know you can postpone this if it's too uncomfortable.

Ellen: I want to do it.

David: OK.

[A long pause, during which DD goes over to Ellen, sits next to her and puts her arm on Ellen's shoulder.]

Ellen: God! I can't believe I'm going to say this.

DD: [hugging Ellen] It's OK.

Ellen: [Emitting a forceful sigh] I want everybody in here to know. [Pause] I cannot believe I'm saying this! [another pause] I want everybody to know that, this week. God! [Pause] This week...I actually thanked that son-of-a-bitch.

[Momentary silence, then laughter, cheers, applause]

Ellen: Not out loud, mind you. I'm sure-as-hell never going to let him know it. But I did it.

What a colossal milestone her painfully funny confession represented! Ellen went on to explain that, during the week, she had been tired and not at her best. Her elder daughter had come to her with a typical pubescent issue that was both age appropriate and annoying. She had offered a possible solution, but her daughter was being obstinate and made a fuss. Ellen found herself impatient with the impasse and on the verge of a verbal explosion. While it was going on, she was thumbing her way through a stack of old mail trying to distract herself and prevent what she knew was going to be a confrontation. As her mood was approaching a boiling point, she happened to uncover an envelope from her husband in which a previously read letter contained particularly upsetting information. Seeing it stopped her cold. She said the effect it had on her was as powerfully repulsive as if he had walked into the room at that moment.

By now she had been working with the waking dream long enough to recognize its significance immediately. She saw her own attitude and her escalating anger as being directly related to that envelope. She said that her first thought upon seeing it was, "That's me!" To her, the envelope was a symbol of her own attitude. All that she found offensive in her husband's behavior—his caustic disapproval and his continual attempts to give himself the upper hand at her expense—she now saw as her own behavior with her daughter. Armed with this understanding, rather than confronting her child in a burst of fury, she took this young girl by the hand, led her to a spot on the sofa, put her arm around her and had a calm, sincere mother-daughter talk during which she listened to her daughter—really listened—and alternately offered some simple suggestions of how to solve their disagreement. In the course of this conversation the impasse was resolved, the black clouds of her daughter's mood blew away, and as the now-sunny, bouncy eleven-year-old got up to leave, she turned and gave her mother a quick peck on the cheek. Ellen said the gesture probably took no longer than the blink of an eye, but it communicated more to her than all the mountains of legal verbiage she had been obliged to labor through during the last year-and-a-half.

This was a moment of profound understanding for her: She was angry with her daughter and on the verge of a verbal explosion. Instead, she recognized a clue provided by a piece of mail and understood that, metaphorically, the letter represented her own caustic behavior pattern. She shifted her attitude, and the change resulted in a positive, deeply satisfying outcome. She understood that she took control of and resolved a situation that, normally, she would have felt overwhelmed by. And most extraordinary of all, she knew that the important tip came from a waking dream: an envelope that, viewed literally, meant little, but metaphorically, revealed her own attitude with its resultant counterproductive behavior.

Ellen's divorce ordeal was not to last much longer, but she didn't know that yet. For her, it was life as she had come to expect it over the last eighteen months, except that she now had a new tool at her disposal. During the following weeks she began to pay closer attention to the connection between her own attitude and the extent to which something reminiscent of her husband would make an appearance. There continued to be some quietly dramatic moments as Ellen saw that there was, indeed, a link between the two. For example, she related a reaction she had to a particular phone call. She heard the telephone ring, but before she answered, she saw from her caller ID that it was her husband. Her abdominal muscles immediately tensed in a familiarly unpleasant manner. She, nevertheless, had the presence of mind to do a quick inventory of her own thoughts. As a result, she made a hasty attitude shift, and after calmly picking up the phone and saying hello, heard her husband's rather caustic, "Oh, it's you. I must have punched the wrong button on my fast dial." Instead of engaging her, he hung up without another remark. In the past, a comparable incident would have signaled the beginning of a confrontational exchange. It would have continued until her husband was certain he had left her exhausted and demoralized. Now, though he was anything but gracious, the interaction was over almost before it began.

This incident, taken out of context, would mean little. A few weeks earlier Ellen would have explained it away as no more than a coincidence. It could be argued, for example, that her husband heard her answer the telephone in a different tone of voice, had a change of heart and chose to hang up when it had been his intention to provoke her. However, since she only uttered a single word, that seems unlikely given his past belligerence. No, something else was going on. Within the context of events taking place in Ellen's life over the past several weeks, this incident was part of a growing, recognizable pattern: Whenever Ellen successfully lived the new attitudes she was working so hard to adopt, her life became smoother; when she forgot and slipped back into old habits, it became bumpy once more. And all of this was transpiring in an arena larger than one she had personal influence over.

There is no question that Ellen had control over some of the events transpiring in her world. Changing her attitude and having a meaningful talk with her daughter after seeing the envelope is a good example. She did that all on her own. Far more difficult to explain away was the continued, consistent behavior of her husband's attorneys who left her in peace when she successfully lived her life from her new perspective.

In Chapter 12, I quoted philosopher Joseph Campbell who said that, if you follow your deepest, most heart-felt urgings—your bliss—"doors will open where there were only walls." Campbell did not mean this in a poetical, head-in-the-clouds way. He meant it as an adage to be relied upon during practical, day-to-day living. I, too, have seen this phenomenon at work in the waking dream: Live from a state of wholeness within yourself, and there is a kind of magic that takes place where things and events completely out of your control suddenly work in your favor.

Certainly, much of what we experience when we change our attitudes and live from a healthier emotional place within ourselves can be attributed to our own more constructive approach to life. But there is something else at work as well. As stated in Chapter 5, Carl Jung wrote about the a-causal connecting principle where he described how two seemingly unrelated phenomena in life influence each other in ways they ought not to; they are not governed by cause and effect. I would amend that observation to say that they are not governed by cause and effect that can be viewed and tracked as an objective experience. However, it has been my observation in working with the waking dream that the connection between these two seemingly unrelated phenomena is causal; there is a cause and effect. It's only that the cause and effect are expressed metaphorically in dream symbols. Taken literally, one can find no logical connection. However, metaphorically everything falls into place. When understood from that perspective, the connection becomes clear, and it can be a powerful phenomenon: Change yourself for the better, and the metaphor presented to you by the world shifts to reflect who you have become. To quote once more from Campbell, if you live in a manner that is true to your most cherished convictions "the universe will conspire to assist you." The phenomenon that takes place is bigger than you are. It involves a strange kind of manipulation on the part of life that is designed to be of help. As Ellen was beginning to discover, it can be potent.

26

The conclusion to Ellen's ordeal.

Ellen was both amazed and elated to discover that there was a connection between an attitude she expressed and events that she would normally consider outside her realm of influence. She was really "getting it," and was beginning to understand that she had a degree of personal power in the midst of this morass that she never had imagined possible. By changing her thought patterns, and thus, changing herself in any given moment, she was beginning to influence the circumstances in her surroundings on an incident-by-incident basis. She understood that she had affected her husband's remarks by her own attitude shift. In the end, she finally comprehended that it was she who was controlling these events, not him. What a revelation![12]

In certain respects, Ellen's experience was similar to Anne's, the woman in Chapter 6 who had repetitive dreams that were mildly erotic. Once Anne got over her sense of guilt and understood the symbols, she actually welcomed these dreams because they brought a message with them that was helpful; they offered a useful prompt when she was falling into old patterns. Ellen began to see that she, like Anne, could use her husband's intrusions in the same way. Whenever he made his presence felt, she could turn her attention to her own attitudes to see if she was falling into old ways of thinking and behaving.

Anne's dreams were sleeping dreams; she had them at night when one would normally expect to be dreaming. By contrast, Ellen's repetitive dreams of her abhorred husband making unwelcome appearances in her life, were waking dreams. Yet, like Anne, she got to the point where she no longer needed to dread them. Rather, she actually grew to welcome them. Their only purpose was to deliver a metaphoric dream message, one that she now understood was a

---

[12] The idea of the universe conspiring to work with you is a theme central to the teachings and philosophy of Joseph Campbell. He referred to the concept repeatedly in his writings and lectures; it appeared in many variations throughout his work. For an excellent overview of the concept as he intended it, see the introduction to his book Pathways to Bliss, pp. xxiii-xxiv.

communication she wanted and needed to hear. The message acted as a course correction, offering her a tip-off when she, like Anne, began to revert to old habits. As a result, the repeating waking dream symbol of her husband's caustic appearance in her life changed from one she despised to one she actually was grateful for. That was what she meant in the dream class when she uttered her supremely memorable line, "I actually thanked that son-of-a-bitch."

How did her ordeal finally resolve itself? Now that she had learned to see her estranged husband's behavior as an aspect of herself, was there a dramatic Hollywood-movie ending to the conflict?

Not at all; what happened was so understated as to seem anticlimactic: While Ellen's ordeal was going on, her own attorney had been quietly involved in unrelated talks with an old friend from law school. The two lawyers had decided to form a mutual practice, the agreement being consummated at about this time. Ellen's attorney briefed his new colleague on Ellen's case, and the two decided to work on it together. Something about this new lawyer's calm, understated style brought a different dynamic to what had, up until then, been a contentious process, and within a matter of weeks an agreement was reached. It was that simple. Undoubtedly Ellen's husband could sense that he no longer was getting the kind of gratifying reaction from her that he'd once had. All that was needed was a catalyst, and once it appeared the pieces fell into place.

A coincidence? Luck? Inevitable? Only a question of time? The resolution was so calm and casual it could almost be accepted from those points of view—except, perhaps, for explaining the timing of the new attorney's serendipitous appearance. Was it "just one of those things," to borrow from Cole Porter? Certainly there was an aura of wonder at the way events played themselves out to Ellen's advantage. But if one tries to explain it all away using words like "random" or "chance," then I would take issue with that conclusion. Anyone who really studies these occurrences can't help but see that they are systematic. Over the years I have marveled at their impressive consistency. Certainly Ellen would argue that the outcome had a great deal to do with the changes she made in herself. For her, there was an unmistakable cause and effect.

Monetarily, Ellen did not get everything she had originally demanded from the divorce settlement, but she got enough, and she also took away something much more valuable than material assets. Working with the waking dream had now become an indispensable habit. Perhaps she was not as wealthy in her bank accounts as she might have wished, but within herself she discovered a treasure of life-assisting tools far more precious than any currency.

27

Not only Ellen, but anyone can tap into his innate wisdom through dream metaphors.

For many years I lived in a small New England town. While offering the ambiance of a rural community, it was also large enough to boast a local newspaper which, from time to time, sponsored a creative writing contest. One of the weary editors whose job it was to act as a judge for these literary events, was once heard to grouse, "Sometimes I think the world would be a lot better off if fewer people 'followed their bliss.'" She was paraphrasing a famous remark made by philosopher, Joseph Campbell.

Although one can certainly sympathize with this journalist as she waded through reams of enthusiastically submitted but otherwise mediocre prose, her gripe actually demonstrated a misunderstanding of Campbell's statement. She is not alone in her error. Many people think that Campbell was urging them to discover a particularly stimulating interest or occupation to help them lead more fulfilled lives. While pursuing an engrossing interest certainly can be part of one's bliss, it is really only the means to a greater end. Here is Campbell, himself, lecturing on the subject.

Bliss is...that deep sense of being present, of doing what you absolutely must do to be yourself...Your bliss can guide you to...transcendent mystery, because bliss is the welling up of the energy of the transcendent wisdom within you.[13]

"Your bliss can guide you to...transcendent mystery...to the transcendent wisdom within you." Achieving that inner wisdom implies a personal commitment to exploring something within yourself that is much deeper than an absorbing interest. It suggests contact with some internal pool of understanding. It indicates getting in touch with a source of innate knowledge that isn't necessarily apparent until one looks for it—like the clues Ellen began to pay

---

[13] Campbell, Joseph; Pathways to Bliss; p. xxiv.

attention to, the ones that seemed to come from outside of herself—the phone call from her husband, for example. These incidents were waking dreams that would normally be considered random events. Yet, as this book has argued, she seems to have created them from within her own psyche. Ellen could not have understood their significance in her life without dedicating herself to a particularly rigorous self-examination.

In the preceding chapters, we saw how Ellen did dedicate herself to this degree of scrutiny by seeking help and support in the midst of her divorce ordeal—through analysis of her waking dreams with the aid of a dream group. At first she felt completely victimized by forces beyond her control. By the time her personal experience of hell had ended, however, she had successfully reassessed how she interacted with life, especially in regard to how much control she could exert over the uncomfortable circumstances that presented themselves to her. She became proactive rather than reactive when she discovered her personal power through the dream. Her stress level plummeted, and she exuded confidence. In other words, perhaps for the first time in her life, she tapped into her own inner source of strength, her own "transcendent wisdom." Like Ellen, anyone can do this.

By no means the only technique, analysis of dreams can be an excellent way to gain access to the kind of self-awareness Ellen found. Among other things, she learned that dream metaphors—to be further discussed in the next chapters—are continuous. They exist night and day for anyone who chooses to recognize and use them—to live life with far greater understanding and personal strength.

PART FIVE:

THE EVER-PRESENT METAPHOR

Part Five examines the ubiquity of dream symbols, suggests a way to isolate the important ones, and explores why dreams seem so disjointed.

28

In a dream interpretation session, one learns to respectfully and courteously offer ideas and suggestions about dream symbols.

It will now be helpful to revisit the one and only rule that I enforce without exception when I work with an individual, or when a group of people gets together to discuss dreams. This rule, first introduced in Chapter 6, is the inclusion of the all-important phrase, "If this dream were mine..."[14]

To ensure a safe and respectful environment in a dream class, participants are required to use this phrase whenever someone wishes to express an idea about another person's dream. As a result, both speaker and listener know that the comment is being offered gently as a possibility to be studied and pondered, nothing more. It reminds the speaker that he really doesn't know whether or not his thought is relevant to the dream. It also puts the dreamer on notice that no one is going to do his work for him. Rather, he is being offered suggestions to consider, but only he can reach conclusions in regard to their validity. It tends to take a session or two for people to get into the habit of prefacing their comments with this simple phrase, but with occasional reminders, the practice becomes second nature and is done as readily as saying "please" and "thank you." After all, like those expressions, it is a form of courtesy.

In dream classes, self-expression is encouraged and quietly nurtured. All attendees are routinely urged to comment on some aspect of the dream currently being discussed. As a way of urging dreamers to begin thinking in terms of symbolism and dream metaphor, each individual is asked if a particular symbol or section of a dream brings strong thoughts or ideas to mind. Everyone gets a chance to

---

[14] Only recently did I become aware of the excellent dream work of Montague Ullman and his nearly identical phrase, "If this were my dream." While his purpose in using this phrase is somewhat different than mine, nevertheless, his use also serves to distance the speaker slightly from the dreamer. Courtesy and non-invasive interaction in group dream classes and seminars is essential. Any responsible dream facilitator will take pains to assure the comfort and psychological safety of someone sharing a dream among peers.

contribute. Once the concept catches on the enthusiasm tends to rise, and the decibel level goes up accordingly. In these circumstances it is vital to remember to respectfully address others.

Imagine a different kind of scenario: You are attending one of these evenings for the first time—drawn to it despite your misgivings—because of a nagging, uncomfortable dream that has been recurring in your sleep once every few weeks for the past several years. The symbols are unsettling, their meaning seems ominous—usually because, at this point, you are taking them literally—and you are embarrassed about sharing anything so unsavory with a group of strangers. What if, after you finally overcome your reticence and lay your most private inner turmoil open for examination, you are bombarded by a slew of noisy opinions, personal dream philosophies and animated insistence that someone in the class has "the answer" to your dream's secret meaning? This would not only be intimidating, it would constitute an invasion of privacy. In extreme cases, even when these dream interpretations are offered enthusiastically with the best of intentions, it can have a demoralizing effect on the dreamer. So, in our sessions, every effort is made to avoid this type of exchange, and a simple way of ensuring that nothing like it takes place is to use the phrase, "If this dream were mine."

Rarely does this cause problems, but it did happen once, and it led to the following confrontational exchange I had with a serious new attendee named Travis. Another class member had just finished relating a sleeping dream about his house catching on fire, and we were, as usual, going around the circle with participants offering lively—often insightful—suggestions as to what the dream might be about. When it came to Travis, he launched right in, a little bit too aggressively as it turned out:

Travis: It's obvious that the house in your dream is your own...

David: Whoa! Whoa! Whoa! Sorry to cut you off, but nothing is ever obvious in a dream. Whenever we talk to someone about their dream experience, we have to understand that we can be wrong. That's why the first few minutes of class were spent reminding everybody to say, "If this dream were mine." It's a simple enough conversational device, and it puts the speaker in the role of a guest in someone else's private experience rather than as some sort of infallible dream diagnostician.

Travis: But saying that would be completely out of character for me.

David: Well, that may be so, but you still need to let the dreamer know that you're not trying to railroad your point of view. I suggest trying it once.

Travis: I wouldn't do that because it's something I would never say. I'd be presenting a false front.

David: OK. But in my book that's all the more reason to give it a try.

Travis: What do you mean?

David: If it's out of character for you then it means you have to think about it first, and that's a great way to remind yourself that you are being invited into someone else's private thoughts rather than expressing your right to be there.

Travis: But coming from me it would sound stilted and unnatural.

David: Well, Travis, you have a choice. You can either choose to say nothing, or if you have an idea you want to express, you need to say or do something that conveys your understanding that you're making a suggestion and nothing more. "If this dream were mine," is a simple way to do that, but if you've got a better idea, you're welcome to give it a try.

Travis was clearly annoyed at having to acquiesce to what he considered our kindergarten-mentality approach to this issue. As it turned out, his ideas, when he eventually got them out, were good ones, and he got lots of support from the group, but after that night he never came back.

It is always disappointing to lose a class member, especially to something as seemingly trivial as the prefacing of comments with "If this dream were mine." However, there is no compromise on this issue. This simple phrase provides a safety net that makes sharing intimacies acceptable. It enables great freedom of thought. Our evenings are endlessly entertaining and delightful. Nearly everybody involved takes pleasure in nurturing a timid participant beyond the limits of what he might ordinarily express, but it is always within set boundaries.

Many years ago, I had my own lesson about stepping over the line when I became too enthusiastically insistent in regard to someone else's dream. It was during a class in Southern California, and a young man named Tim was relating the following waking dream:

Tim: I'm at this restaurant on the beach in Malibu. The weather's gorgeous. I'm eating outside on the deck, and since it's evening, there's a sunset. I'm thinking that the Pacific is as blue as I've ever seen it. And that, plus the colors in the sky, make everything look really beautiful. The food's great, and I'm full and feeling satisfied. There are seagulls circling around over the water. They're noisy and seem happy. I'm feeling drowsy and content. I'm just about to close my eyes for a second when I watch as two gulls break formation, gracefully fly over the beach and swoop near me. One lands on a chair close by, and the other actually ends up perching right on the far edge of the table where I've just finished eating.

It is helpful to understand that the people in this particular class were together because they shared a common spiritual outlook. While it is true that dream symbols have different meanings from person to person, it can also be the case that people with similar life perspectives, mystical or otherwise, can share symbol definitions. Therein lies potential disaster, for to assume that everyone is sharing them—as I was about to do—is to make a colossal error in judgment. I was planning on telling the class what Tim's dream was about; I saw it as simply confirming what I assumed was a consensus of thought.

When all was said and done, my interpretation, which fortunately I never stated, was partially correct. But that, as it turned out, wasn't good enough. Here's what I came up with: To a person with a spiritual viewpoint, food can mean nourishment of the soul. The food at this restaurant in Malibu was delicious and satisfying. The environment was idyllic, like a paradise.

The ocean is often interpreted as the subconscious. But for this group, the ocean was an expression of things deeply sacred because, in their tradition, it is a metaphor for God. The sun was setting in a dramatic and colorful show, implying that the day (a cycle) was ending in a breathtaking display. There were "happy" birds. Any flying entity that soars and transcends the earth can be viewed as celestial, and Tim, who was feeling content and drowsy, was actually being visited by one of these beings. Indeed, the whole dream seemed to be taking place in a blissfully celebratory Elysian setting, and as I listened, I found myself sighing in vicarious contentment. My assumptions, however, were abruptly shattered.

I remember thinking that this dream was so obvious we really didn't need to work our way ponderously through all the symbols; we could simply congratulate Tim on his spiritual milestone. However, as the facilitator, I needed to set a good example. While making a half-hearted show of keeping up appearances, I nevertheless broke one of my own rules and asked a quick question in which I lumped several dream symbols together. "So Tim: Tell us about eating delicious food on the Malibu beach with a setting sun in the background, surrounded by soaring creatures." Tim didn't hesitate for an instant. "It reminded me of Hitchcock's movie The Birds," he answered.

It is not easy to render me speechless, but that is exactly what Tim, in total innocence, succeeded in doing.

For those readers who may not have been impressionable teenagers in 1963, Alfred Hitchcock, the great English film director, was a master of the psychological thriller. In this particular film, decades before the advent of digital special effects, Hitchcock and his team somehow managed to make it appear as if great swarms of non-predatory birds, many of them seagulls, were all congregating at one particular town for the sole purpose of attacking and killing the human beings who lived there.

That Tim could associate his balmy Malibu restaurant meal with this frightening movie was a jolt that forced me back to a more thoughtful exploration of his experience. As it turned out, Tim's dream was an expression of something mystical in his life, and the birds were (metaphorically) spiritual entities. But far from lulling him into a state of drug-like oblivion, the seagulls were there to wake him up, even if it meant making him feel uncomfortable and threatened. That was precisely the point. He'd allowed himself to be seduced into a state of cosmic tranquilization by the "great meal" he had been enjoying. True spiritual experiences are rarely about being anesthetized. Rather, metaphysical exploration has the effect of increasing awareness, of making one more sensitive. Tim was telling himself to snap out of his trance; he needed greater spiritual vigilance.

As repeated throughout this book, one of the basic assumptions in the interpretation of any dream—waking or sleeping—is that all facets and symbols of the dream are parts of the dreamer. That was as true for me as for anyone else that evening. The Malibu restaurant meal was certainly Tim's dream, but he wasn't the only one being admonished to wake up. I could see right away that his dream was as much aimed at me as at him. And it made its point. On those extremely rare occasions when I still feel like cutting corners while working on someone's dream, my memory of Tim and his birds is all I need to entice me back to the straight and narrow.

Imagine if I had pressed my interpretation on Tim and insisted that I was correct. The whole purpose of this dramatic and beautiful waking dream would have been wasted. It doesn't matter who is making the suggestion. The individual offering an idea to a dreamer can be the most experienced and astute dream analyst in existence. But we all make mistakes. The phrase, "If this dream were mine," is a way to acknowledge our limited and potentially flawed perception, and to give the dreamer the freedom to accept or reject our suggestion.

29

My own dream metaphors are explored.

When I first became interested in dreams I wasn't particularly good at remembering them. In those days I had no knowledge of the waking dream, so it was a question of trying to hold onto sleeping dreams while I mentally traveled from slumber, through the twilight of awakening, and finally, into full consciousness. This exercise was anything but easy. It is impressive how many subtle states there are between deep sleep and full alertness. Often I'd manage to remember the details of a particular dream, bringing it into what I thought to be a full state of wakefulness. Yet sometimes, no more than a single minute after my declaration of success, the dream would be gone. This became so frustrating that, after an aborted attempt or two, I managed to devise a way around it. I set my alarm so that it would go off every two hours all night long. At first I kept a pad next to my bed to record my dreams as soon as I was awakened by the alarm. That was unsuccessful. On the few occasions when my pencil actually managed to make contact with the paper, the scribbles were illegible. Next, I tried a variation, using a small recording device. That was better. In the morning I would treat myself to the mumblings of my barely intelligible voice. With rare exceptions, the verbal cues, albeit vague and confusing, were enough to bring the night's dreams back to vivid recollection.

What I began to realize was that, even when I remembered multiple dreams from the same night, and even if the symbols were significantly different from dream to dream, when these symbols were dissected and interpreted in the usual fashion, each dream said nearly the same thing as the one before it—and after it. This is a scenario common to the vast majority of dreamers I have encountered. Dreams are a reflection of the dreamer at any given moment. They speak in a symbolic language which includes plays on words and also puns. However, most of them communicate with us in metaphors. This banter is incessant; it never stops. Through much of the night during sleep—especially during periods of R.E.M. (rapid eye movement)—then during the daylight hours, sleeping and waking dreams offer an ever-present depiction of our state of mind. This is constant, seemingly for our entire life.

I kept up my experiment for several months. As I conscientiously continued to set my alarm, I noticed that this action was becoming superfluous. After a while my body simply got into the habit of waking itself just long enough to drone something into the microphone. Then I would fall right back into a deep sleep. Every morning I would have a vague recollection of my night dealings with the tape recorder and eventually felt no sleep deprivation or inconvenience. This was in contrast to my condition at the beginning of the whole experiment when I felt as if I were continually jet-lagged.

The hardest part was finding the time during an otherwise busy day to go through quantities of dreams, analyze pages of symbols and try to make sense of it all. Since there was so much duplication in the various dream messages, I began to have serious doubts about the continued usefulness of the whole project. Then one morning I flipped on the tape machine and heard myself say things that I absolutely did not remember. That was spooky enough to use as an excuse to end the ritual for good. Yet, I had learned plenty.

I understood for the first time why sleeping dreams can seem so disjointed, and why, when they are analyzed, the symbols don't always appear in chronological order. As we'll see in upcoming chapters, this knowledge became useful in the classes I taught. I could help others understand the structure of typical dreams and how dreams present themselves to us.

30

A dream class discussion makes sense of a disjointed dream.

From time to time the vast majority of us have dreams that are confusing. Their plots seem illogical, or they jump from one apparently unrelated detail to the next. When examined literally, they make no sense. Yet when they are viewed as metaphor, and these metaphors are interpreted using the five steps suggested in this book, their messages suddenly become clear. The most disjointed dream stories come into focus, and all at once, deliver a message that is of importance to the dreamer.

To illustrate the phenomenon of a dream's illogical plot line and how it can be brought into clarity, we'll now eavesdrop on a typically lighthearted dream class the way it would naturally be progressing. In this segment, a student named Jed is relating a sleeping dream he had a few nights before. (Note the respectful use of the phrase "If this dream were mine . . . ")

Jed: Well, you know how it goes. All I remember is a snippet or two.

David: Let's have it anyway.

Jed: What I remember is in two parts. In the first half, I'm installing a window in a brand new house. The construction isn't quite finished yet, and I know that the window is the last part to be done. I also know that the house is mine, and I'm going to be living in it. I'm working outside the house, holding the window unit in place, and as I look through the glass into the house, what I see seems weird. The house looks completely lived in. There is carpet on the floor. There are books and knick knacks on shelves. There are signs that someone has been there because stuff is lying all over, like someone was in a hurry to be somewhere else and didn't clean up.

Then the scene shifts to the second part I remember: I'm in the middle of a really busy intersection with lots of traffic. I'm the traffic cop. I'm on one of those round platforms a couple of feet off the ground so the drivers can see me better. I'm waving my hands around, telling people to stop and go and turn. And there are lots of cars, except that they don't have normal car roofs. Instead, the roofs are pushed out really high—kind of like small double-decker busses—except that the top halves are in the shape of human brains.

AA: The top halves of the cars look like brains?

Jed: Yeah. And that's it. That's all I remember.

AA: How weird!

BB: I have this image of brain matter being pliable like gelatin. Were the cars wiggling around all over? [laughter]

Jed: I don't think so. That didn't seem to be the focus of the dream.

David: OK. Who's got some ideas?

CC: I think the "brains-on-the-cars" image is really interesting. When I imagine brains, I tend to think they represent thinking itself, or maybe thoughts. And they're on cars so they seem to be moving around. If this dream were mine, I'd wonder if I was doing some thinking. Or maybe there was something on my mind.

AA: Yeah. You're directing the traffic. It seems like there are all these thoughts racing around. If this were my dream, I'd be looking at whether some ideas were churning in my head.

Jed: I don't know that the cars were really racing around as much as there were a lot of them.

BB: But weren't you having to deal with the traffic coming from all directions?

Jed: Yeah.

BB: So maybe AA's image still works.

David: What about the first half of the dream?

EE: Wait a minute! I still want to talk about brains. I think you guys are putting a kind of negative spin on this. Maybe Jed's just cooking up some plans. I mean, the traffic's under control. There's no sense of a crisis. If this dream were mine, I think I'd just ask myself if I were throwing around some ideas.

David: How about it, Jed. Are you throwing ideas around?

Jed: I think I've always got something going on inside my head. I don't think my brain ever stops. In fact, it can be a problem sometimes. So, I guess, in a general sense, what everybody's suggesting rings true. But I can't really think of anything specific in my life right now that particularly fits.

David: Well, let's keep going. How about the house?

BB: The window's kind of cool. Maybe it's a kind of protection. You can see out and you can see in, but there's this invisible barrier that keeps out the bad weather.

EE: Yeah. And the bugs. [laughter]

David: "Bugs" is an interesting word.

AA: The window lets in light but it keeps out the stuff you don't want inside.

CC: Unless something crashes through it and breaks it.

David: Jed, is there any sense of danger in the dream while you're installing the window?

Jed: No. I just know it's the next thing I need to do.

EE: Oh! I got it! [excited] You're putting in the window to keep...

David: [interrupting] If this dream were mine ...

EE: Right. [collecting himself] If this dream were mine I'd wonder if I had all these thoughts racing around that were trying to get into my space, my house. I mean, in the dream you said the house was yours and that you already live there. But now you're kind of putting up a protective barrier. It lets you see in and out, but it gives you some privacy, some kind of distance from all those car-thoughts in the second half of your dream.

David: Nice! What do you think, Jed?

Jed: [smiling] It's funny you should say that. I started meditation classes about a month ago at the gym. I thought it might slow down some of this brain activity.

David: And?

Jed: The weird thing is that, before tonight, I was thinking seriously of quitting. I couldn't see any results.

AA: Don't you think a month's a little soon for that kind of decision?

Jed: Probably.

David: According to your dream, would you say the meditation's having a positive effect?

Jed: [chuckling] Maybe so.

This discussion continued for some time. The class was fascinated by the dream's many symbols: the carpet, the knick knacks on shelves, the "stuff" lying around the nearly-finished house, the concept of actually living in an unfinished space, the idea of leaving things scattered about haphazardly because one is in a hurry to "be somewhere else." Then, another set of symbols followed: standing in the middle of an intersection on a traffic cop's elevated platform. Directing the traffic of cars whose tops were in the shape of human brains.

All of these details enhanced and clarified the dream's message to the point where everyone, including Jed, was confident of the interpretation we had already reached: Through his new meditation classes, Jed was rebuilding the place he lived inside himself. He was putting up a protective barrier—the window—so that he could view his mental distractions—brainy cars—from a greater distance. He would be aware of them, but like a traffic cop, he would be in control of them. The dream seemed to be advising him to be patient, that the meditation was having the desired effect.

The symbols, when examined literally, made little sense, especially when the two halves of the dream were put together. Yet, when Jed saw and owned the symbols as metaphors, they told a story with a message that was logical and helpful.

No one seemed surprised at the two disparate sets of symbols. First, there was a house being worked on, then there was the scene with "brainy" traffic. The class members had worked their way through plenty of equally bizarre dream scenes and nobody was daunted. What did bother them, though, was that the dream seemed to be backwards. The solution to Jed's problem—putting in a window so that he could see, but otherwise be separated from what he didn't want—seemed to come before the problem had been stated—trying to keep control of a myriad of brainy cars.

Some wondered if maybe dreams were typically disjointed, and that it was only our order-obsessed minds that demanded a logical sequence of events. I believe that concept is essentially correct, but I offered them another idea to consider as well—that dreams remembered in their entirety could also have logical plots.

I told them about my dream recording experiment. I explained that when I was really keyed into remembering multiple dreams that had occurred during a single night—remembering those dreams as a whole—I was surprised at how straightforward the story lines were. What often made them seem disjointed was remembering only bits and pieces. I suggested that this was, perhaps, what Jed had experienced. Maybe the small amount of dream time he was able to bring back to waking consciousness consisted of the tail end of one dream (about houses) followed immediately by the beginning of the next (about brainy cars).

Ultimately these details of dream character make little difference, except to remind us, as stated earlier, that the metaphors never cease. The instant one dream is over, its message is redelivered by the next set of symbols. Even though the latter symbols may have no seeming relationship to the former, their metaphoric communication is related. That process goes on until the dreamer makes a subtle—or dramatic—shift in his thinking or consciousness. Then the dream symbols change to reflect a new circumstance.

31

Three dream categories are introduced, illustrating how to tell if a dream is important.

How does a dreamer know when a dream is important? This is easier to determine with sleeping dreams than with waking dreams. The majority of us remember only occasional parts of our sleeping dreams—at most an entire dream or two. When we remember them it is usually because these dreams leave an impression on us. That, in itself, is a sign of their importance. We simply forget the rest of our less-significant sleeping dreams.

With waking dreams, it is different. Because we are awake, it is possible for us to remember the minutiae of daily life. Everything coming into our awareness is a dream. When a dreamer first understands this idea, it is tempting to see the smallest event as worthy of interpretation. It can become almost a fixation: "Oh! I just tied my shoe. That's a waking dream." True. But is it an important one? Those who try to live their lives analyzing even the most insignificant detail, soon become overwhelmed.

For this reason, over the years I have isolated three types of waking (and sleeping) dreams that are important and worth paying attention to. In all three categories, if the dream is truly consequential, the common characteristic is that it leaves the dreamer feeling unsettled—sometimes upset—and is difficult to forget.

1) a dream that is shocking
2) a dream that is bizarre
3) a dream with a symbol that occurs more than twice

Waking dream examples in each of these three categories have already been presented: Austin was shocked by his malfunctioning cruise control. A young woman had the bizarre experience of falling on her face while she was on a walk looking at a plum tree. Gwen had repeated encounters with her obnoxious restaurant co-worker.

Keeping these categories in mind, it will be useful to look at some new dreams. While we will eventually look at all three dream types, the next few chapters concentrate only on the first two.

32

The first category of a dream is discussed—a waking dream that is shocking.

In New England I had a friend, Stan, who was a computer specialist. Like many "nerds" he spent a good deal more time inside his own head than in the gym. Of slender build, he often gave one the impression that the slightest breeze might simply waft him off to some distant computer Nirvana. He was clearly brilliant. From time to time he would engage me in a discussion, trying enthusiastically—albeit unsuccessfully—to demystify some technical computer puzzle he was unraveling. Brilliant though he was, he had to pay his bills, and he did so by acting more mundanely as a computer service technician.

Stan made house calls in the rural countryside, and many of his customers lived down dirt or gravel roads. Thus, in the course of a year, he would put a good deal of mileage on his battered car.

One evening, I received an unannounced visit from him. He asked to work on a waking dream that had left him shaken. What follows constitutes Step 1 of our dream interpretation session as it transpired that evening: Relate the dream.

Stan told me that on the day of his incident he had arrived at his customer's home early and chose to take a walk before his appointment.

Stan: It was one of those great October days, so I decided to take a jaunt along the road. It was quiet and beautiful with all the fall colors. I had been walking along for just a few minutes when, about 50 yards ahead, two huge Doberman Pinschers bolted out of a driveway I hadn't noticed, and charged straight at me. I remember having a bunch of thoughts in the few seconds it took them to race across the distance. First, I remember thinking that the animals were absolutely beautiful. But the rest of my thinking was all about being scared out of my mind—real terror. I knew that even one of these dogs could easily knock me down. I realized that there wasn't a thing I could do about it, and I knew that my life was probably over. I froze in my tracks and just waited to be torn to pieces.

But the two dogs, aggressively running toward him at top speed, suddenly skidded to a stop directly in front of him, started wagging their tails furiously and began a studious nasal examination of his trousers and shoes, which bore ample olfactory evidence of his house cat. Stan said he was so terrified he doesn't know how he managed to stay upright. He only vaguely remembers his subsequent service call and thinks a guardian angel must have driven him home. When he arrived at his house, he had a stiff drink, took a hot bath and went straight to bed even though it was mid-afternoon.

Stan's dream encompassed not only the part above that he narrated in the first person, but the descriptive paragraphs immediately before and after. Ultimately, he and I dealt with every aspect of his waking dream. For the purposes of this discussion, we will limit our analysis to only the most important symbols that Stan related above in his own words.

Stan and I quickly dealt with the next part of the dream interpretation process: Step 2: Isolate the symbols.

1) Taking a walk along country roads
2) Charging Dobermans
3) Waiting to be killed

Then, together, we began Step 3: Interpret the symbols as metaphors. What follows is part of our dialogue.

David: Tell me about walking along country roads.

Stan: Ohhh! They're my favorite places to walk, so beautiful and quiet.

David: Tell me about charging Dobermans.

Stan: My God! It took me days to stop shaking.

David: OK, but try to tell me about them.

Stan: [thinking] They're attack dogs. Aggressive. They're used in police work and dealing with bad guys. Stuff like that.

David: How about these particular Dobermans?

Stan: I thought they were going to kill me, but I guess they were pussycats.

David: OK, if you thought they were going to kill you, then tell me about your life ending.

Stan: My life ending? I have no idea. What happens when your life ends? I don't think anybody knows.

David: Good! Good work!

We took a short break, and then I read his symbols back to him in Step 4: Retell the dream, using and owning the metaphors.

David: Stan, if this dream were mine, I'd say that there's a part of me that consists of "my favorite place to walk." This part of me is "beautiful and quiet." But while I'm there, another part of me seems to come "charging out of nowhere." This is a part of me that's an animal. It's "beautiful but aggressive." It's the part of me I use to "police" myself, to keep the "bad guys" that live inside me under control. I'm sure this part of me is going to "kill" me, although I don't really know what that means. But, as it turns out, I am mistaken. This part of me only seems to be "aggressive; it's really just a pussycat."

I must say, I was taken aback by Stan's "bad guys" imagery. He's such a congenial, soft-spoken fellow that it is hard to imagine him with an inappropriate bone in his body. However, that was only my own perception of him. Seeing the discrepancy between what I perceived and the direction his own thoughts seemed to be going was added incentive for me to be careful in my subsequent remarks when I introduced Step 5 Explore the dream's relevance in your life.

David: Stan, if this dream were mine, I'd wonder if there was some kind of conflict going on inside myself right now. It seems like my peace and quiet and beauty are being invaded by something aggressively animal—something that seems to be looking for bad guys and may be about ready to kill me off. But it also seems to be a big charade. It turns into a pussycat. Does any of that make sense?

Stan needed no further prompting. He explained that he had recently returned from a computer conference in New York City. While mingling with his colleagues he had been impressed, in fact startled, by the discrepancy between what many of them were earning and his own relatively meager income. While the seminar was mostly a forum for the latest gadgetry and computer innovation, he attended a lecture as well, and this experience seemed to confirm his deepest fears. The gist of the speaker's presentation was that those who were attracted to computer work often tended to have a difficult time interacting with people. As such, it was easy for them to be taken advantage of. It was important to make certain they weren't cheating themselves, especially if they were self-employed. There followed a graph of recommended hourly charges with the admonition that, if one's own business was functioning significantly below the recommendations, one was not only doing a disservice to oneself, but to the trade of computer maintenance in general.

Stan felt alarmed, chagrined and even thought he might be on the road to failure. He came home determined to change his life. He felt he should be more assertive, that he should live up to the expectations of his New York colleagues, and that he had the right to be more demanding than he had been up to now. He was adamant that he would correct these disparities.

All the while, at the back of his mind was the nagging understanding that his customers had chosen this rural lifestyle for the same reason he had. Namely, they preferred the natural beauty and slower pace of country living, and frankly, the reason he was charging less for his services was because his clients simply couldn't afford more. If he wanted additional money he knew he should leave the countryside and relocate to an urban area where a higher pay scale was appropriate. Simultaneously, his mind led him in the opposite direction: he took the recent New York admonition seriously, and he decided it was time to act on his own behalf and raise his prices. This particular service call, where he encountered the dogs, was to have functioned as his first assertive step forward.

As he learned the hard way, it was all a big bluff, and somewhere inside himself he already understood that. If he raised his prices he knew he'd lose many of his customers, actually putting himself in a worse rather than improved financial position. He was well aware that he'd made the decision long ago to live a lifestyle that allowed him a degree of freedom and comfort in his eccentricity. This lifestyle suited him so well that he wasn't about to give it up. Yes, it meant a more modest standard of living, but this had never bothered him before. In fact, it hadn't bothered him until the New York convention. So here he was, trying to come charging out of nowhere like an aggressive animal to confront and defeat parts of himself he had always been perfectly at peace with. Instead of being content, he had found fault with his way of living. He had turned his love of freedom, comfort and eccentricity into negative qualities. In his own words, these qualities were now the "bad guys" whom the Dobermans were attacking.

As stated above, there was much more to the dream: the part about the battered car with lots of mileage on it, and the statement about not knowing what happens when life ends. There was also the remark about the guardian angel, and Stan's action of coming home, having a stiff drink and going straight to bed in the middle of the afternoon. These turned out to be issues that, although related, were long-term and philosophical in nature. More immediately, from his waking dream with the dogs, Stan got the most important message being delivered: Be true to yourself.

This was a prime example of a dream that was important enough to the dreamer that it shocked him. He will not soon forget either the dream or its message!

33

The second category of dream is discussed—a waking dream that is bizarre.

Because I have exposed so many of my former students' dreams to literary scrutiny, it seems only fair to tell one on myself—a waking dream. What follows happened to me a year or so after the destruction of the World Trade Center twin towers on September 11, 2001—the infamous "9/11." Many Americans will recall that, even a year after that event, it was a particularly tense time in the United States. Many of us felt that we needed to respond militarily to this aggressive and unspeakable act of terror. Others among us were outraged at what we perceived to be a rash and poorly-prepared scramble to react. Like everyone else in the country, I had my own opinions, and they were strong ones. If I expressed them openly, I would frequently be embroiled in an argument with someone who passionately disagreed with me. Over time I found myself becoming increasingly adamant and entrenched. The more I encountered others whose points of view differed from my own, the more enraged I became. My fury was starting to influence most of the facets of my life, and there was even some indication that it was affecting my health. But I was still doing nothing to change. Like so many others in the country, I was simply letting it eat into my peace of mind and influence how I went about living. It was a perfect scenario for an important waking dream event.

Against this backdrop, my wife, Patti, and I flew to California to celebrate the birthday of a friend who, as it happened, was also rejoicing in his third year of remission from a near-fatal case of Non-Hodgkin's Lymphoma. Patti and I rented a car and drove to our agreed-upon meeting place, the Monterey Bay Aquarium. We found the parking garage and chose a spot near the elevators, because Patti had suffered a bad fall years before which made walking an ordeal. For this reason, I would also carefully pull into public parking spaces hugging the driver's side of the car to the painted line in order to leave her a little bit of extra room to exit the vehicle.

We spent a glorious, celebratory day at the aquarium, not only enjoying the impressive exhibits, but attending some of the docent lectures as well. Our excursion was a welcome respite, although I found myself alternating between joy at our friend's recovery and a sense of nation-related anger and concern.

Fortunately, celebration won the day, and Patti and I headed back to our little rental car in high spirits. Just as we reached the vehicle, a large SUV pulled into the space next to us on the driver's side. Having made it a practice to give Patti extra room on the passenger side, I was used to negotiating the kinds of narrow gaps this causes on my side. I simply slid up to my car door which I opened with what would have been an appropriate force for the relatively heavy doors on our own car. For this little rental, however, it was excessive, and the door almost flew out of my hand as it went crashing into the side of the neighboring vehicle.

My happiness changed instantly to remorse, and I turned quickly to apologize to the woman sitting on the SUV's passenger side. I had only enough time to catch the look of disgust on her face before she jerked her head away to avoid making eye contact. At the same time, the driver got out, and marched around to where I was standing, clearly a man on a mission.

"Didn't anybody ever teach you to be careful?"

"I'm really sorry, I hadn't meant to..."

"You just slammed your door into my car."

"I know. I was trying to..."

"And look at how you're parked!"

"Yes. It's true, I'm..."

"There's plenty of room in that space if you just drove like you knew what you were doing."

"I realize that. It's only that..."

"You know, the trouble with people these days is they don't think."

"I'm sorry."

During the course of this heated exchange we were both examining the side of his car, and had we not been in the midst of an altercation, I think each of us, independently, would have expressed genuine surprise at its pristine condition. I had expected to see a sizable dent, and subsequently, to be handed a wallet-wilting invoice for cosmetic auto body work. The fact is, there was not a scratch to be found, and since any expression of forgiveness was absent, there was nothing to do but drop the issue and stiffly go our separate ways.

So, drop the issue we did. Except, I was fuming during the whole drive back to the airport and all through the subsequent flight home. I was still angry well into the late hours of the night when I finally fell asleep. When I awoke the next morning, my anger hadn't subsided. I remained incensed, but I was also weary of my obsession with the whole silly incident.

Being emotionally invested in the experience, it took me time to distance myself from it. But that morning it finally dawned upon me that this was a classic case of an important waking dream. It fell into the category of a quirky and bizarre experience, one that was difficult to let go. At that moment, I finally calmed down, found my way to a comfortable chair, and went to work on the symbols.

I am no different than anyone else. Owning the metaphors of any uncomfortable dream that comes into my life is objectionable. I had already related the dream to myself many times. It was easy to isolate the important symbols, and that was part of the problem. I knew that, eventually, after interpreting the symbols as metaphors, I was going to have to own the metaphors, which meant identifying with my adversary. I'll be perfectly frank: I didn't like the SUV guy at all. He struck me as abrasive, hard, opinionated, unbending in his attitude and beliefs, too quick to draw conclusions, only partially informed, unnecessarily confrontational . . . At that point, I started to laugh. I was, of course, heatedly describing myself.

I made a thorough examination of my own life, my own attitudes and the issues that were of paramount importance to me at the moment, and it didn't take long to put the various pieces together. This was Step 5: Explore the dream's relevance in your life. What was I being adamant and unbending about in my life? Politics! Suddenly it became apparent that my angry fixation with the condition of my country, a rage that I had been carrying around inside for such a lengthy time, was being graphically characterized right back to me in my waking dream. I was the one who was being "opinionated and unbending." I was the one picking the fight.

As I sat there in the morning pondering all this, the dream message began to sink in. I could feel myself let go of the whole obsession, and my breathing became deeper and more relaxed. It would, of course, take time to let go of it completely. Nevertheless, I got up out of my comfortable chair, headed into the kitchen to make my breakfast and found myself walking with a bemused smirk on my face. Thinking about that man and his SUV, I caught myself borrowing a line from Ellen: I actually thanked the son-of-a-bitch.

I continued to ponder this dream over the coming days and weeks—as we also will in the following chapters—paying particular attention to some of the other symbols: There was the light-weight rental car and my inadvertent violence to a neighbor's vehicle. There was the absence of a dent where there ought to have been evidence of one. There was the friend, celebrating his birthday, whose cancer was in remission. There was the aquarium itself with its lectures and beautiful displays. Finally, the symbol that caused me to chuckle the most was the SUV driver's remark that, "The trouble with people today is they don't think." While none of these symbols significantly altered the essential message, they each added to the richness of the dream.

When I am analyzing a dream for the first time, I insist on examining each part. This time, I invite the reader to try unraveling the above symbols on your own. Use the phrase, "If this dream were mine," and make it a conversation with yourself. Start with something like, "Tell me about an SUV," and go from there. If you feel like it, put yourself in the role of a dream class member. It isn't necessary to attempt a breakdown of the entire incident. Pick a symbol or two, something you find yourself drawn to. Simply let your imagination go; you might surprise yourself.

PART SIX:
SELF-IMPOSED CONFLICTS

Part Six suggests that we participate in the creation of our own dream symbols—both sleeping and waking, both pleasant and unpleasant.

34

When life is unfair, perhaps it is so, by design.

There are many philosophical and spiritual teachings that predict the dawning of a new age with more understanding, fewer injustices and hardships, less anguish, higher states of consciousness, and above all, peace. There is, for example, an impressive esoteric community in northern Italy called Damanhur that has geared its whole social structure in anticipation of this inevitable life shift.[15] Also, I recently listened to some taped lectures by Deepak Chopra and Wayne Dyer in which they trumpeted the arrival of this emerging time.[16] Eckhart Tolle is another world teacher who feels that a global change is in progress.[17] And here is what author and cosmologist, Neale Donald Walsch, has to say on the subject:

There is a slow chipping away happening. We are gradually stripping the block of granite which is the human experience of its unwanted excess, as a sculptor chips away to create and reveal the true beauty of the final carving.[18]

Those are hopeful assessments and predictions, but not all luminaries agree. Sant Thakar Singh, a master of the Sant Mat path, for one, often disparaged the physical world, referring to it as a wilderness.[19] From his perspective, although there always have been and always will be pockets of enlightenment, the world as a whole remains a dissatisfying, unjust environment. In this discouraging perspective, Sant Thakar is echoing a sentiment that is millennia old and was perhaps most famously stated 12,000 years ago by King Solomon:

In my opinion, nothing [in the world] is worthwhile; everything is futile. For what does a man get for all his hard work? Generations come and go,

---

[15] Merrifield, Jeff: Damanhur; pp. 13-20

[16] Dyer, Wayne and Chopra, Deepak' "Creating Your World The Way You Really Want It To Be"; Cassette #2, side 1.

[17] Tolle makes repeated references to this global shift in a 2009 lecture entitled "Awakening in the Now" taped at UCLA. www.eckharttolle.com

[18] Walsch, Neale Donald: Conversations With God—Book 2, p. 234.

[19] Singh, Thakar: The Way of Life, p. 90

but it makes no difference...everything is unutterably weary and tiresome.[20]

For my own part, I am hopeful that the first group of teachers mentioned above—the ones with a more optimistic view of our future—are correct. Perhaps we are, indeed, plodding our way haphazardly toward a better world.

But I also must look at the current, more discouraging world realistically; I cannot simply put my life on hold while I wait for a dramatic global sea change. Thus, I have chosen an approach to living that is based on my own assessments, ones made after years of studying the consistency of metaphoric patterns in daily events: It has been my observation that life—at least for now—is supposed to be the way it is—unfairness and all.

Our current passion for a purer form of existence is not new. I was brought up in the Quaker tradition which, among other tenets, has strong pacifist leanings. I gained a great deal from that way of life; it was constructive, infectious, and it imbued me with a profound sense of the worth of humankind. Then, during my Junior year in high school, I wrote a term paper about a man named Elias Hicks, a nineteenth-century Quaker mystic who formed his own splinter group. Hicks' action so upset the peace-loving Quaker community as a whole, that many of its members loaded their firearms and started taking pot shots at each other. Similarly, Jesus, "the prince of peace," has had numerous wars started in his name. Mankind yearns for a utopian existence then consistently falls on its face. We talk ad nauseam about "fixing" life. We want to end wrongfulness, eliminate distress and lift up the down-trodden. Yet, in reference to the last chapter, it was precisely the outrageous nature of my little incident with the SUV driver in Monterey that caused me to grow. It was its injustice that forced me to be aware of my own toxic anger.

Uncomfortable situations like the one discussed above, are placed directly in front of us from time to time and are often considered insurmountable obstacles. They seem to come into our lives as a form of cosmic behind-the-scenes manipulation deliberately designed to entrap us. We find ourselves in situations that, had we known about them ahead of time, we would have done our best to avoid them. It has been my observation that these kinds of uncomfortable

---

[20] Solomon; The Living Bible—Ecclesiastes 1-2, p. 508

circumstances are deliberate, put directly in our way, blocking our path so that we are forced to deal with their distressing intrusions into our affairs. From a traditional point of view they seem unmerited. We are minding our own business, and suddenly life surprises us with an unexpected problem, giving us no escape. From an every-day, "normal" view of living, intrusions like this are horribly unjustified. However, if one can step back far enough to consider them from a different perspective and then interpret their language—the language of metaphor—the injustices can be experienced as lessons. We might be greatly surprised that, rather than being offended, we are actually receiving a gift.

We, especially in the West, are geared to looking at life "objectively" rather than considering upsetting events as metaphors. As a result, we have concluded that something is radically wrong with existence, and that it needs repair. Yet if life is broken, as we seem determined to believe, we need to recognize that it has been in that state for a very very long time.

I am suggesting an alternative point of view. Perhaps life is not broken but is that way by design. Simply look into the past. In any given era some form of order is established—occasionally with justice but more often without it. Despite competition, this order rules supreme for a while. Then something comes along and successfully challenges it. It breaks down in turmoil, and a new order replaces it. That has been the relentless case throughout recorded history, and there is overwhelming evidence—astronomical, geologic and, more specifically, fossil—to suggest that the same pattern has been repeating itself since the dawn of time. Is life really broken, or is it that we simply prefer not to acknowledge its nature? And, if it's not broken, then what about us poor miserable creatures caught in the middle of it? Instead of doing battle with what we deem problems, I am suggesting that we pull back and view life from the perspective of the dream metaphor, seeing purpose in what appears to be random injustice. We could then consider our own possible unconscious participation in the obstacles that present themselves, seemingly unwarranted, into our lives. As a result, life might take on new meaning with new opportunities for self-discovery and personal growth.

35

It seems that we, ourselves, help create life's apparent inequities.

The last chapter ended with the suggestion that we might participate, unconsciously, in the unfair circumstances that life seems to force upon us. Over the next chapters, and indeed, throughout the remainder of the book, I will offer examples of waking dreams that are so specifically tailored to the dreamer that it is difficult to imagine how they could be arbitrary events randomly placed into the dreamer's lap. And whether we are dealing with irate SUV drivers or confronting far more intense circumstances, the perceived unfairnesses align themselves into consistently coherent "messages," absolutely relevant to the personal crisis being faced.

One thing is certain: when we deal with these crises as metaphor, we have far greater control over the outcome than seems logical. Perhaps this ability to have influence over these events begins earlier than we would imagine. Maybe it starts with their creation. Let's follow this train of thought in a further examination of my SUV incident in the parking garage of the Monterey Bay Aquarium.

Until I worked through the dream symbols of my encounter with the SUV driver, the incident left me agitated. The reader may recall that I was fuming, and I was not alone in my distress. The occupants of the other vehicle were upset as well. Certainly I had done them an injustice. I had angered them, and they had every right to feel violated. The driver made a point of expressing his opinions in regard to my shortcomings, and since I was given no opportunity to respond in my own defense, I felt demeaned. It seemed that we had stirred up a dust devil of ill will. As a result, all of us left the scene without a sense of resolution.

My fuming unleashed a slew of "if only" thoughts. If only the woman hadn't turned her head away so quickly, she would have been aware of my apology. If only the driver had let me explain my parking arrangement, he would have been more understanding. If only we could have had a chat and talked about the celebratory reason for Patti's and my being there in the first place, the hard feelings would surely have dissipated. If. If. If.

The fact is, none of those things happened, and what's more, I would like to suggest the idea that they weren't supposed to happen. Perhaps the incident came into being especially to teach me something.

Let's assume for a moment that some exchange had taken place which removed the sting and brought an amicable ending to the whole affair. Would I still have dropped my rage at national politics, and once again, brought peace to my life? All indications were that I was becoming increasingly mired in my own anger which, without some figurative (or even literal) slap in the face, would have continued unabated. That would have been toxic.

We all know people who carry these kinds of attitudes around with them continually. It colors everything they do, every decision they make, every thought they have. In some cases it even makes them physically ill. By contrast, I had a day or two of unsettling discomfort, then managed to pull myself away from the issue long enough to see it from a different perspective. Finally, I put it to rest. My adversary turned into my teacher; my attitude toward politics evolved into strongly and constructively held beliefs. The dust devil simply lost its swirl and vanished into nothing. Yet before it did, it created enough turmoil to force a closer look at something unpleasant in my life. It seems I needed that dust devil. And who created this particular storm in my life? I am convinced that I did. The incident—both its manifestation and its resolution—was specific to me and my needs in the moment. It is difficult to imagine it being an arbitrary, random event. Someone or something made it up, tailored it to my needs, and made certain that it was brought to my attention. Who else but some unconscious facet of myself? Perhaps at some mystical level there was the assistance of a higher power, but I certainly acted in concert with it.

After decades of analyzing hundreds of dreams—in four languages and on three continents—I have become convinced that, somehow, we participate in the creation of our dream symbols. This process is, of course, obvious in regard to sleeping dreams; while we are asleep, we subconsciously create our symbols. But I am referring equally to waking dreams. I do not understand the mechanics, but it has become evident to me that it is we, ourselves, who invent the waking scenarios—fair or unfair—that confront us on a daily basis. It is as if the imaginative process we go through with our sleeping dreams, where we clearly fabricate images, transfers itself to our outer, objective waking lives.

36

The most poignant learning seems to take place more often through a distressing situation, rather than a pleasant one.

Both waking dreams highlighted in the last chapters were easily remembered because of their intensity. Stan's encounter with Dobermans (Chapter 32) was shocking. My confrontation with the angry SUV driver (Chapter 33) was not only bizarre, but aggravating. However, when a dream tries to instruct in a friendly fashion, it can easily be ignored. Here is a personal example: Once I was in a hurry to finish the dishes. While the garbage disposal was grinding the last bits of debris, I picked up a brand-new bar of soap to wash my hands, but it slipped through my fingers, slid down the drain, and was then chopped noisily into slivers along with the remains of egg shells and broccoli stems. That was surprising—and funny! And it fit all the criteria of the second important dream category: the bizarre dream. It was significant, too—something about being heedful not to squander a good "cleansing" through subsequent haste and carelessness. The only trouble was that, since I found it amusing, I didn't pay close attention to it until the usefulness of its warning had passed. It was only months later when I was quietly pondering dreams that I remembered this incident and realized its value. Humor is disarming. It puts us in a good mood, and we prefer to remain lighthearted. By contrast, analyzing a dream symbol takes work, and it tends to be the last thing we want to do when we're enjoying ourselves.

Why is it that, so often, we seem to require a disagreeable circumstance in our lives to grow? I don't have an answer to that question, but it seems to be the case. The idea of obstacles put in our way—introduced in the last chapters—demonstrates how our subconscious self undermines our conscious will. We become seemingly-inadvertent participants in a circumstance we would never choose if left to our own resolve. In other words, we "push" ourselves into an unpleasant situation in order to grow. It is as if we need to be shaken out of our complacency to move forward in our understanding. If, as also stated in the last chapters, the unfairness of life is deliberate, then it seems as if the inclusion of unpleasant situations is a necessary part of the growth process. We learn something important, then live our lives with that new understanding as a reference point.

Why can't the same learning be accomplished without distress? Sometimes it can. But there is a tendency, when life is comfortable, to "stay where we are" in our own awareness. If the message being delivered comes in the form of a pleasant waking dream—humorous, enjoyable, delightful—we will usually take it at face value and miss the nudge. In many situations it is a displeasing jolt that pulls us forward to a new level of awareness. It seems that we often need distress to grow.

37

Everyone's dream is uniquely his own, and that results in a paradox in which we are obliged to live in both an objective and a subjective world.

It is a vital and fascinating aspect of the dream phenomenon that every participant has a unique perspective on what happened. If several people take notice of a particular waking dream, each of them is going to be confronted, symbolically, with something of themselves. This is an idea that I now want to explore further in regard to my SUV incident.

After I had worked through the dream symbols, I was finally able to ponder this incident from a calmer, more appreciative perspective. At that point, what I wanted more than anything, was to find the driver again, sit down with him over a cold beer, and ask him to "tell me about" having a total stranger slam a car door into the side of his vehicle. I had worked on this incident from my own perspective to understand what it was trying to tell me. But what about the other participants in this affair? Did the dream bring the same message to the SUV's driver, or to his wife?

In any incident involving more than a single individual, there are multiple dream perspectives, but there is often no opportunity to discuss the event from different points of view. The incident might have left one player so rattled that, by the time nerves are calmed, the other players are long out of the picture. Or, the people involved may simply want to avoid discussion. Sometimes an event involves a person with an inanimate object or an animal, like my bar of soap or Stan's Dobermans.

On the few occasions during dream workshops when I have actually been able to explore multiple facets of a single, momentous event, asking more than one observer to "tell me about it," the results have been astounding. The same shared and dramatic event, when analyzed as a dream by two or more involved individuals, almost always results in poignant symbolism for each of them, however the symbolic message being delivered is unique to every person.

This is one of the reasons why, in a group setting, I am so insistent that participants offer suggestions only; I make certain that they never assume the rightness of their ideas. Ultimately, the only person who can correctly analyze a dream is the dreamer himself, because each dreamer sees an event—literally sees it—in his own way.

As an example, I once had a conversation with a police officer about a local traffic accident that had made the news. There had been a dispute because the two involved drivers disagreed about who was to blame. I asked the policeman why there was any doubt, since several bystanders had witnessed the crash. He responded: "When perfectly normal, ordinary people get excited, it's amazing what they think they see." This was a problem for the policeman, as it would be in any situation where a consensus was required.[21] Yet for me, the different manner in which people see a given incident presents the key to a more subjective—but equally helpful—way of dealing with life.

It has been my observation that we exist in a paradox. We certainly live in an objective reality, such as the traffic accident the policeman was trying to make sense of. But we simultaneously live in a subjective reality as well, the world of dream metaphors. The Western view is that life is an objective experience, and that our subjective impressions keep us from having a clear vision of the world around us. However, throughout the book we have seen how people who understand the waking dream have used that same subjectivity as a useful tool to gain vital insight into their lives.

Successfully straddling the objective and the subjective, those seemingly irreconcilable truths, can be a tall order, but it can be done. Working with the waking dream is one of the easiest ways to begin exploring this dual realm. For those of us in the West, seeing life objectively is second nature. But working subjectively with the waking dream is not complicated. As we have seen repeatedly, the dream interpretation techniques are simple; they are exactly the same for both sleeping and waking dreams. It doesn't matter who we are, our station in life, our level of education or the belief system we were born into. We all have equal access to this subjective phenomenon and to the powerful understanding it can provide.

---

[21] There are a number of books available describing the inaccuracy of witness accounts in courts of law. An excellent one is True Witness by veteran litigator, James M. Doyle.

38

The third category of dream is discussed—a waking dream with a symbol that occurs more than twice.

Eunice was a waitress that my wife, Patti, and I got to know and love while we were living in New England. She had only a rudimentary formal education; her principal learning came from the school of hard knocks. She had been physically, emotionally and verbally abused all throughout her childhood, and the result was a combination of low self-esteem and a dogged determination to prove to her family, to life, and mostly to herself, that she was worthy of respect. She went about this through relentless hard work and a street-honed outrageous wit that, despite her limited vocabulary and earthy manner of speech, was more imaginative and humorous than many professional comedians. When she waited tables, uninitiated new customers would frequently be taken aback at her demeanor and caustic remarks. Once they got the hang of the game, though, they almost invariably came back for more.

The game, itself, would start with a vaguely insulting quip from Eunice, and the idea was not to shy away in alarm, but rather, to match her wit, gibe for gibe. You knew you had scored a point when Eunice, herself, would dissolve into her own hoarse cadence of machine-gun laughter which could be heard all over the restaurant. It was like dinner theater without the cover charge, and people loved it. As might be expected, sometimes the antics went beyond decorum, and Eunice would be called in by management for a little chat. Those were gentle reprimands for sure; the fact was, Eunice was great for business. She consistently packed the house, and her employers were anxious to maintain the status quo. "Uh oh! Got chewed out again," Eunice would whimper in mock remorse and then would explode into laughter.

This kind of behavior could easily have led to jealousy and resentment among her restaurant colleagues, but they all knew that if any one of them got into trouble, Eunice would be the first one there, making herself available and going well out of her way to try and make things better. Beneath the scratchy demeanor, she had a heart of pure gold, and at one time or another, everyone had experienced it.

Sadly, all this represented only half of Eunice's life. The other half, the darker portion, exacted its toll. Never having had a stable male role model, she had no idea how to attract, let alone maintain, a relationship with an appropriately loving and caring man. She had a covey of children, each one sired by a different "lover," each lover having been more reprehensible than his predecessor. So the pattern was being passed on to the next generation with her kids, now teenagers, alternately in jail or at home, having their own babies and being abusive to their mother. The whole scene made you want to pull your hair out and start screaming. You had the feeling that if Eunice would have had a fair shake in the first place, her strength of character and desire for right living would have made her a completely different person. If. If. If.

When Patti and I got to know her, she had—atypically—been in a relationship for quite a while, this one having had the distinction of being formalized in an actual marriage. Because of that, she was trying extra hard to make it work and maintained a brave face. From time to time, though, she would let a remark slip that hinted of domestic problems. "I'm gonna give him 'til April 23rd, 1979 to get his act together."

I have made up the date simply because I can no longer remember what it was, though the remark was classic Eunice. The date, itself, represented some arbitrary point of decision making, the veritable line drawn in the sand, except that it was at least eighteen months into the future. When I reacted in dismay at her self-abusive generosity of spirit and suggested that she was giving her husband an inordinate amount of time, Eunice's response was typical. "Yup. That's me: a Libra. Always sittin' on the fence." One thing about Eunice, she either made you laugh or cry—sometimes both at the same time.

For those who might be perplexed by Eunice's remark, people born under the seventh astrological sign, Libra, symbolized by the scales of justice, are reputed to weigh decisions with great care. However, because a Libra person presumably sees the value of all sides of an issue, that person can sometimes have difficulty committing to a course of action. Without discussing the validity of astrology in general, the description, in Eunice's case, was apt. She was giving her husband a year-and-a-half to magically grow into an acceptable level of behavior before she was willing to intervene.

Fortunately, she did not wait that long. She was already confiding bits and pieces of her problems, an indication that things were worse than she let on. Eventually she had a heart-to-heart talk with my wife, Patti, who suggested that, since she had been taking my class, she treat her situation as a waking dream and discuss it with me. At Eunice's own suggestion, she and I took a walk in a lovely park where we could have privacy in the midst of pleasant surroundings.

This was her story: It seemed that the unemployed ne'er-do-well whom she had chosen to marry, in addition to adding to her financial woes by being an extra mouth to feed, was also demanding an inordinate amount of sex, often several times in the course of a single day. In the morning, when she was preparing for work, he would want sex. When she came home, tired after a long busy stint at the restaurant, he would demand it again. If work involved a double shift, which left her completely exhausted, he would still insist on a repeat performance. Then, as if that weren't excessive already, as they were falling asleep, he would put in his order for a night cap. This kind of thing had been going on for months and had left her bewildered, drained, angered and ultimately demoralized. She didn't want the marriage to fail, so she was trying to be responsive to "his needs." By contrast, he refused to take her own state of affairs into consideration, and to make matters worse, he seemed unwilling to contribute constructively to their partnership in any way. Suggestions that he go find a job always resulted in his waxing eloquent about some grand money-making scheme that wasn't "quite lined up yet"—and, of course, never would be. Eunice was beside herself, and didn't know what to do.

This certainly qualified as a waking dream with a repeating symbol. While trying to be sensitive to Eunice who had confided so much embarrassing intimacy to me I, nevertheless, told her what I thought.

David: Well, Eunice, if this dream were mine, I'd wonder if a big part of my marriage was about me getting screwed.

My remark took her aback. She had chosen the walk in the park expecting the symbolism of her dream to unfold gradually, like some magical flower opening petal by petal as she had witnessed similar situations in class. She had prepared herself to follow a string of images that seemed unrelated, ones that would eventually reveal a metaphorical vista and show her some unexpected and beautiful truth. There was no question that she was given the truth, but she was not prepared for its bluntness; dreams can be like that.

To fast-forward to the end of the story, Eunice spent no more time considering alternatives. In a matter of days she booted her husband out of the house!

39

Even if we are poorly educated—like Eunice—life, with our participation, customized our dream symbols to our culture and our language.

In the 1940s American author, Conrad Richter, wrote a trilogy called *Awakening Land*, which is about the beginnings of the American western expansion. In the second of the three novels, Richter tells the story of a poorly educated settler named Luke Peters who decides to abandon his new stake in the Ohio territory and return east. Luke has been given an omen—albeit a misspelled one—a group of letters which he has seen in the sky:

Right off he knew the Lord was talking to him. The Lord had written letters in heaven spelling out a warning for him to read.

"What did it spell?" George Roebuck asked.

"F-A-M-I-N! Luke Peters told him.[22]

On hearing this news, Luke's more-learned fellow settlers nearly dissolve in mirth. They have no problem with the idea that he has received a heavenly sign; it is entirely plausible that he has read letters in the cloud formations sending him a message. However, what they find absurd and cannot abide is the idea that the Lord, in all His omniscient glory, would have misspelled a word, leaving the final "e" off "famine." For that reason, they dismiss the warning as fraudulent and continue to think Luke's concern is hilarious, until they are nearly starved out of their new settlement the following summer.

While *Awakening Land* is a work of fiction, this incident poses an important question in regard to the waking dream: When "the Lord" wants to deliver a message to someone who is poorly educated, is He willing to misspell words if, by doing so, the recipient can understand Him better? Or, to pose this inquiry as a generic question: How personalized are the symbols of waking dreams? Is there a "correct"

---

[22] Richter, Conrad; The Fields; p. 44.

way that they come to us, one that is the same for everyone? Or, are symbols individualized to the recipient's own understanding of life?

It has been my observation that life tailors waking dream symbols to fit the understanding, language and culture of the dreamer. This is one of the reasons why I am so convinced that we, ourselves, participate in the process. While it can happen that the meanings of certain dream metaphors are general and can apply to more than one dreamer, it is also true that other symbols are uniquely suited to only a single dreamer.

Eunice's poignant "screwed" metaphor is an excellent example. In her vocabulary—indeed, in American culture in general—a crude, derogatory slang term for sexual intercourse has taken on the additional meaning of someone being swindled or defrauded. How common is this usage? Is it archetypical, existing worldwide, or is it specific to certain societies?

I decided to find an answer to that last question by asking any foreigner whom I happened to meet (and who I felt would not be aghast at the subject matter), if they had a comparable expression in their own language. In a totally random query, this is what I found out: Dutch, Russian, French, Italian and the East Flemish dialect (including Antwerp and Brussels) all make similar use of their slang term "screwed" or "fucked." It is both an impolite, sometimes pejorative reference to sexual intercourse, and it is also an insulting word that means being cheated. In the West Flemish dialect, however, it doesn't exist.

Further, I talked to a woman who had grown up in the eastern half of Germany when it was part of the Soviet Union. Her native language is, of course, German. But living in an occupied country, she was obliged to study the language of the occupiers, and she and her peers heard plenty of crude talk from soldiers stationed in her region. She and her friends simply could not understand this obscene Russian reference to sex. It made no sense to them. "I think the German preoccupation with cleanliness," she explained, "makes it much more likely that a comparable and insulting German expression would be a reference to filth, not to lovemaking." Where she grew up, there was no expression, "This is really screwed," meaning that a situation is faulty and does not measure up to expectations. On the other hand, the German expression, "This really shits," is ubiquitous.

A physician born in Saigon had this to say about the use of the word screwed: "Nine out of ten Vietnamese wouldn't even understand your question." In this doctor's culture, if someone feels cheated, he directs his indignity either at an individual whom he is convinced is responsible for the fraudulent circumstance, or he aims it at the gods in general. It seems that, in the Vietnamese language, there is no casual epithet for feeling swindled, certainly none that is also a synonym for sexual intercourse.

The above examples point out the extent to which life will tailor its waking dream symbols to fit our own cultural imagery. Eunice's waking dream experience falls into the same category. She somehow collaborated with her physical environment to manifest an individualized set of symbols which would have been incomprehensible in many places throughout the world. Yet they spoke specifically to her. For Eunice, these two seemingly unrelated ideas—having sex and being victimized—came together from the single word "screwed" as a powerful metaphor. It was poised on the edge of her conscious awareness, easily interpreted, waiting to be understood as a sign to change her world.

The idea that life will metamorphose to cater to our needs and cultural understanding is an extraordinary concept. It suggests that, somehow, the universe with our help, will create a waking dream symbol specific to our culture and language as well as to our personalized needs.

40

Sometimes a dream symbol is too poignant to tolerate.

Perhaps the reader noticed that, in dealing with Eunice, I avoided repeating her dream back to her in the usual way. Instead of saying, "There is a part of me that is screwing myself," I implicitly suggested that, "There is a part of my marriage that is about me being screwed." This difference, at first glance, may seem subtle, but it was important. It allowed Eunice to maintain some distance between herself and her dream. A symbol can sometimes ask for more change than the dreamer is capable of. The dreamer might understand the dream concept in general, work with its principles, recognize examples and deal with it cerebrally. But when it comes to personalizing a particularly powerful symbol, there are times when that symbol can cause a dreamer to feel overwhelmed.

This was true for Eunice who would have been the first to agree that, in her dream, she was describing herself. She was well aware of her shortcomings. She knew of her tendency to undermine her personal affairs. She fully understood that it was her responsibility to prevent the tangles she found herself perpetually ensnared in. Yet, over the years, she demonstrated her inability to keep these knots out of her life. Conceptually, she had no problem understanding that she was "screwing herself" with her entrenched habits. Yet, it is one thing to understand a problem and quite another to act on it successfully. Had I reminded her, through her dream, that her impossible marriage was nothing more than a symbol of her own state of consciousness and that her dream was telling her that she was causing all of her own problems, it would have served no purpose but to reinforce her sense of inadequacy. Instead, I allowed her to project, to hold her dream at a distance, attributing its message to a circumstance outside her consciousness so she could blame her marriage instead of herself.

As a rule I've admonished readers to be accountable for their dream messages, even when those communications are unflattering and painful. Yet in my encounter with Eunice, I broke my own rule; I quietly let her avoid taking full responsibility for her own dream symbol. Why did I allow this exception? Is there a valid circumstance when it is preferable for a dreamer to look outside himself to work through a dream?

I have seen evidence to suggest that when a dreamer simply can't cope with the severity of a symbol's implications, he can successfully work through much of the issue by dealing in a more literal fashion with the metaphor itself. Eunice's example is a good case in point. While she may not have absorbed the entire metaphoric message about victimizing herself, she rid herself of her predatory husband, and that was certainly an improvement.

And there were other changes that occurred as a result of her work with this dream, even though she held it at a distance from herself. The most significant of them was the shift in her behavior toward men in general. Before her poignant waking dream, her approach to them was destructive to herself. Even though she had wanted to build healthy relationships, she repeatedly found herself in associations that undermined her confidence and her sense of self-worth. Before she worked with her dream, she had no qualms about picking up men and bringing them home, with distressing consequences.

After she worked with her dream, things were significantly different. She began to see her sexual affairs and romantic entanglements in the same light that a recovering alcoholic views cocktail parties. In her own words: "I like guys, and I sure could've used one in the house the other day when the dishwasher was on the fritz. But I guess I don't handle 'em so great." Since that time Eunice has never had a relationship with a man that was more than platonically casual. That change, alone, has made a notable difference in the quality of her life. At times it is certainly lonely for her, and there is a quiet sense of loss. But she feels she has gained more than she has sacrificed; she counts her blessings.

Did she get everything out of the dream that was being offered? Not even close. This dream amounted to an autobiography. The pattern of family abuse, then later self-abuse, was established early on when she was still a young child, and in one way or another, she had certainly been "screwing herself" ever since. Under other circumstances (if, if, if) she might have been less emotionally wounded. She might have been able to face the dream symbol in its overwhelming, devastating entirety, go through extensive therapy and possibly emerge from all this psychological work able to attract a caring partner. Such things happen. But by the time she learned about working with dreams—well into her adulthood—this was an unlikely scenario. Her life habits were set. There was too much history, too many patterns established for her to unravel her past and start again.

So I had a choice. As her dream facilitator I could have decided that the dream message was too poignant, and as such, beyond her capabilities. Instead, I trusted her ability to handle a significant part of it. I broke the rules slightly, allowing her to hold the dream symbol of being "screwed" a little bit further away from herself—to "externalize" it as psychologists would say. I did not demand that she own it completely. Instead, she and I looked at the "man in her life" not so much as a metaphor for her own masculine, assertive/aggressive traits (or lack of them), but as a real person. We didn't say, "Look at what I'm doing to myself." Instead we said, "Look at what this abusive man is teaching me. How can I best deal with it?" It's a subtle difference, but an important one. That shift in approach to her dream allowed her to correct one large aspect of her life, and it made an enormous difference to her.

The founder of the Gestalt therapy movement, Fritz Perls, whom I introduced early in the book, and whose work inspired much of my own, wanted his dreamers to look nowhere but to themselves for whatever conflicts and unease were affecting their peace of mind. I suspect that, on this issue, he and I would engage in a verbal tug-of-war. In Eunice's case, externalizing the dream paid off, and I would not hesitate to help another person in this same way if I felt, similarly, that an overwhelming dream symbol was too much for him to cope with. The trouble with this technique, in general, is that suddenly a Pandora's Box of pitfalls opens up. The moment we start looking outside of ourselves for the cause and the solution to our troubles, we start to confront the world at impossible combative odds.

Who among us can consistently win against everything life throws at us? We may be among the most enlightened, shrewd, capable and lucky individuals on the planet, but there is always some circumstance that can come along that is out of our conscious control, an obstacle that seems insurmountable to us. It can be a grossly unfair event which leaves us positively spluttering in indignation or disbelief—or even pain or illness. We are given the impression that we can't do anything about it. If we try to engage it, we will inevitably lose. On the other hand, if we can learn to own it, remembering that, subconsciously, we created it, we can see the metaphor, understand the message it is working so hard to deliver, and by making internal changes, alter the circumstance, and thus, the dream. By externalizing, we lose the all-important esoteric message: Whatever I perceive, is me.

So, yes, externalizing has its value and its place in the scheme of things, as exemplified by Eunice's experience. But it is a compromise, a last-resort technique. When at all possible, it is much better to own what comes our way—pleasant or unpleasant—and deal with it, knowing that, ultimately, it was not imposed on us by the arbitrary cruelty of life or by forces outside of ourselves. Rather, as we have already seen in so many examples throughout the book—and more still to come—we play a great part in bringing these events into our own lives. No matter who we are, our level of education, our upbringing or our beliefs, these events (metaphoric messages) are gifts we give to ourselves in order to grow.

PART SEVEN:

DREAMS AND THE BLENDING OF OUR INNER AND OUTER WORLDS

Part Seven explores dreams in relation to unusual phenomena, all of which show evidence of a sameness between our inner dream world and our outer waking life.

41

Our dream worlds and our awakened lives are similar.

There is a similarity between our waking lives and our dreams that most of us are unaware of. We tend to view our waking lives as being more logical and ordered than what goes on in our imaginations when we are asleep, where our dream worlds are often disjointed and odd.

But, as we have seen, both sleeping and waking dreams are important and impressively versatile. They contain innumerable truths and can be helpful in many ways. They can offer suggestions. They can be a celebration. They can heal. They can be instructive—or intrusive. They can elucidate shortcomings. They can give warnings. They can involve monsters. Dreams can also point to the future as prophetic. And there are those who say that dreams can describe past lives.[23] Some individuals even claim that dreams can provide travel—so-called astral travel.

There are Western researchers who do nothing but focus on nightmares. Shamans in other cultures take dreams more literally, and use them as tools for promoting mental health. Tibetan Buddhists divide them into three distinct categories and describe each type as having unique qualities.[24] One can even decide that dreams are not important at all, being mostly a random collection of images drawn from one's recent waking life events.

In this book, we look upon all dreams, sleeping and waking, as important messages for our benefit. No matter what the dream content, we use dream symbols and their metaphorical meanings as the simplest and most accessible ways to tap into communications being delivered to us from our subconscious minds.

However, to fully benefit from dream metaphor and dreams in their totality, we have introduced the idea—alien to the West—that there is far less separation between what we experience when we are

---

[23] Stevenson, Ian; Children Who Remember Previous Lives: A Question of Reincarnation; pp. 9-29. 115

[24] Das, Lama Surya; Tibetan Dream Yoga; cassette #1.

asleep and the activities of our awakened lives. As a culture, we tend to consider this concept strange and see little evidence of it.

The purpose of the next few chapters is to suggest that there is more evidence in support of the "bleed-through" between sleep and wakefulness than most of us realize. We will examine a variety of unusual phenomena, including prophecy, intuitive "knowing," and paranormal activities in general. We will begin with a form of dreaming that has been practiced by Tibetan Buddhist monks for centuries. In the West, we refer to it as lucid dreaming.

42

Tibetan monks who practice "lucid dreaming" claim that there is little difference between dreaming, wakefulness and death.

There is a form of dreaming called lucid dreaming that has been practiced for centuries by Tibetan monks. While some dreamers do this naturally, it is a technique that usually must be learned; it involves effort and skill. One of the purposes of lucid dreaming is to take conscious control of dream content. Recently, Western dreamers have become increasingly interested in this phenomenon. There are repeated lectures on the subject at dream conferences as well as blogs on the internet devoted to the topic.[25]

In order to dream lucidly, one learns—over time and through disciplined meditation—to gain awareness and control of a dream during sleep, becoming conscious in the middle of the dream itself.[26] In this conscious state within a sleeping dream, the dreamer becomes like a script writer. He takes control of the dream events, and learns to dictate what will happen in the dream by changing the scene and the characters with whom he is interacting.

Often lucid dreamers start with learning how to manipulate a single aspect of a dream. For example, a dreamer may find himself confronting a monster. He becomes aware that he is dreaming and consciously makes the decision not to be in this scary situation. He thinks to himself, "I am dreaming, and I don't like this dream. I want it to change." He continues to instruct the dream to be different, such as, "I would rather not be here right now." With concentration, the dreamer can learn to transform the dream into something else. His initial efforts may result in controlling only a single aspect of it. However, with practice, he can learn to control many elements of what used to be an unconscious activity. His directives become more specific ("I want to be in a meadow with beautiful flowers."), and his thoughts are enough to bring about this change. As in a movie, the

---

[25] www.world-of-lucid-dreaming.com/lucid-dreaming-blog.html

[26] Norbu, Chögyal Namkhai; Dream Yoga and the Practice of Natural Light; p. 88.

dream scene shifts, and he finds himself standing in the bucolic setting he desires.

According to practitioners throughout the world, the experience of the dream eventually ceases to be an end in itself. Instead, dreaming becomes a means to something else. The focus is no longer on dream content or symbols. Rather, lucid dreamers in the Tibetan tradition use this form of activity to break down the barrier between being awake and being asleep. Eventually, they work toward breaking down a similar barrier between the experiences of waking life and the experiences one has after death. That is their primary goal. They spend time learning to dream lucidly because they believe that if one can learn to be conscious during sleep, then one can be conscious at the time of dying. Acting as a lucid dream script writer, they can constructively influence what happens to their souls in the next existence. Tibetans deliberately go about learning to bridge the divide between the two seemingly separate worlds of sleep and wakefulness. They make the discovery of this understanding a priority; for them, that is the most important reason for working with dreams.

For those of us who may not be at that skill level and have found working with dreams and their symbols an invaluable tool, there is nevertheless an understanding to be gained from the Tibetan view. It is the idea that there is less difference between being awake and being asleep than most of us are aware of. For the next few chapters we will explore instances where individuals in the Western world have experienced ways in which the two realms of daytime and sleep activity begin to commingle. These people have found themselves in circumstances that dissolve the perceived barrier between our inner and outer lives.

43

A thin line exists between waking and sleeping states.

As discussed in the previous chapter, approaches to dream interpretation vary widely. However, one thing begins to make itself consistently apparent: life (and its seeming split into inward and outward experiences) is not as rock solid or as fixed as it appears at first analysis. There is ample evidence that the sleeping dream world—the world of our inner imagination—bleeds into our outer "real" lives. Our inner and outer realities commingle far more than we are usually aware of. It goes on all the time and manifests in many forms.

To provide an example, consider an artist I know who probes deeply inside herself to find images for her paintings. She doesn't think the picture into her mind and then onto the canvas as much as she intuits it into place. These painted depictions have a way of coming true in her life, including a few spooky incidents, one of which involved a death, another a terrible storm, plus a third where she painted a sedan that had crashed into a large, tree-like structure. Shortly after completing this picture, her daughter plowed her Honda into a nearby power pole. This artist's experiences are a prime example of her inner world blending with her outer one.

Another instance of an inner life commingling with the outer happened to the world-renowned concert pianist, Arthur Rubenstein. He was a great interpreter of the music of Frederic Chopin. Once, at a reception after a concert, he was asked if he thought he tended to perform Chopin the way the composer, himself, would have played this music. In response, Rubenstein suddenly felt prompted to go to the piano where he performed a Chopin waltz in a way that he never would have played it, normally.[27] This aroused great curiosity among his listeners: Did he think he had been "visited from beyond" during this strange episode? He answered that he doubted it. He believed that at death there was no "beyond." Even so, the incident made enough of an impression on him that it startled him; he didn't forget

[27] Rubinstein related this story in a Public Television documentary entitled "The Love of Life." This program has never been released for sale or rent to the general public. Thus, I cannot be more specific in my citation.

it; he couldn't quite let it go; he repeated it to journalists. Most importantly, even he would have to agree that his peculiar action was not a conscious decision, nor was it motivated by external stimuli, but by something inside himself.

For many people, the ideas expressed in this chapter are as peculiar as they seemed to Rubinstein. These individuals take a quick inventory of their lives and see nothing to suggest a blending of their inner and outer realities. Nevertheless, I have facilitated dreams with some who held that same point of view, yet with surprisingly little probing, they came to see the bleed-through of inner and outer experiences active in their lives. It is all but impossible to ignore the idea that some inner mechanism is orchestrating events that manifest outwardly as waking dreams. The dreamers who saw no blend of inner and outer realities simply had never made the conscious connection between the two worlds.

44

The nature of prophecy is examined in a climber's dilemma.

In the last chapter, the painter whose daughter crashed her car into a power pole had a vision which she depicted on a canvas. The vision then came true; the painter's experience was prophetic. Prophecy is one of the ways in which our inner and outer lives blend. Let's examine another example of this phenomenon, this time in relation to a dream that seemed to be both a sleeping and a waking one simultaneously.

During a weekend workshop, a dreamer stepped to the microphone and began relating a sleeping dream about an arduous climb up a cliff face. He told how, in his dream, the ascent was about half completed when, from above, a small boulder about the size of a basketball, somehow came loose from its tenuous perch and began careening down the slope, narrowly missing him in the process. He explained how the experience unnerved him, and then, in reverential tones, went on to finish the anecdote as follows:

And you know what? A week later I was in the mountains on a hike and almost exactly the same thing happened. It was just like my dream. I looked up and saw this big rock rolling and bouncing right down at me. That thing must have come within a couple of feet. It was weird—first in my sleep, and then in real life!

Prophetic experiences such as this are held in high esteem. They inspire wonder, and most of us don't know how to relate to them when they occur. This climber felt bewildered by his dream experience partly because he viewed the event with such reverence. I wondered if it might be helpful for him to see his incident in a different light, one that gave it less stature. While acknowledging its validity at face value, the question that remained dominant throughout our subsequent discussion was: Did this sleeping dream come as a warning of a future waking experience, or were both occurrences—sleeping and waking—the same dream that was ultimately about something else?

By asking this question, I was revisiting the same issue I brought up with Jeremy and his armoire in Chapter 9. It is the idea that dreams—both waking and sleeping—are continuous, and sometimes we are given multiple dream experiences with identical messages regarding an issue in life we are working to resolve. Sometimes these dream messages come while we are asleep; other times they are given to us when we are awake. Life seems to make less of a distinction between these inner and outer experiences than we do.

One certainly can't discount the seeming coincidence of having a sleeping dream recur in waking form, especially if this sort of thing happens to the dreamer repeatedly. What is also true, however, is that one can view these dual events as a single dream that occurred twice, first as a sleeping dream and then as a waking dream. It took a while for the climber to acknowledge this possibility, but when he finally did, I made the following remark: "Maybe next time, if you can do the work to interpret your sleeping dream right away, life won't have to give you the experience twice, and you won't have to put yourself in physical danger."

This was a brand new concept for him. It represented an altogether different approach to dealing with prophecy. There was no sense of awe or elitism. Viewed in this manner, these kinds of predictive experiences are simply another way that our inner and outer lives work together to communicate with us. In the climber's case, to explore this idea further, we treated his pair of dreams as a single one: He had already related the dream. Next, we isolated the symbols. For the purpose of the following discussion, we will consider only the two most important symbols: climbing a cliff face and big rolling boulders.

Then, we interpreted the symbols as metaphors, as the dialogue below will reveal:

David: Tell me about climbing a cliff face.

Climber: I've been climbing since I was really little.

David: OK, but can you explain your attraction to it?

Climber: I guess I like the challenge. You're out in nature in the elements, and you have to use your wits, sometimes all your strength. If you get into trouble, it's up to you. I like that part. You have to make decisions, and they have to be the right ones. Otherwise it's bad news. You can get yourself into a jam.

David: Anything else?

Climber: I guess the other thing is that, when you finally get to the top, you sit down and look around and it's beautiful, and it's like the whole world is at your feet. You feel like you really did something.

David: Good. Tell me about big boulders rolling down at you.

Climber: Well it wasn't really a big boulder. Just a big rock. But big enough to kill, that's for sure. It's not like on TV. You don't do some heroic thing and jump out of the way. If you're lucky, there might be a depression you can duck down into. But if you're just hanging on for dear life anyway, there may not be anything you can do except pray it misses you.

Now it was time to retell his dream, using and owning the metaphors. I related his dream back to him in the usual fashion, substituting his definitions for the symbols themselves.

There's a part of me that is a challenge. When I go to this part inside myself, which I like to do—I've been doing it since I was little—I have to use my wits and all my strength. I'm in the elements, and if I get into trouble while I'm here in this part of myself, it's up to me. I like that challenge. I have to make decisions, and they have to be the right ones. Otherwise it's bad news.

But when I do it right, I'm on top. I sit down and look around at this part of me, and it's beautiful. I see the whole world at my feet, and I feel like I really did something.

But now, as I am negotiating my way to this part of myself, I see another part of me coming straight at me. I am in danger because this part is capable of killing me. What's more, there is nothing heroic I can do about it. I just have to hang on for dear life and pray it misses me.

This brought us to Step 5: Explore the dream's relevance in your life. I asked if there was anything in his life at the moment that made it seem as if the exhilaration of "climbing to the top and seeing a beautiful view" was being threatened. He became pensive, stated that he was forty-six years old, had set out as a young man to "conquer the world," but was now finding that his priorities were changing. He wasn't sure how to react to this shift in his view of life. He felt it represented a threat to his original goals. From his comments it became clear that there was a personal issue he was dealing with, one that was directly related to the dream subject.

So which was it? Was he having a prophetic sleeping dream to warn him about an imminent and dangerous waking experience, or did he have two dreams with nearly identical content elucidating a personal conflict? In our discussion, we concluded that both things were true.

45

The down side of the prophetic experience is considered.

Prophecy can be a precious gift. It is one way that certain individuals can pierce the illusion of the separation between our inner and outer worlds. When these seers are particularly adept, they can be of great service.

But this experience is not always a pleasurable one. A dreamer named Paul, for example, found his frequent prophetic visions upsetting, especially when his predictions involved others. He abhorred the responsibility of informing friends, colleagues and sometimes complete strangers of happenings he had seen in their futures. He was perplexed about the extent of his obligations under those circumstances. When he said nothing to them, it seemed unconscionable and wrong. When he dropped subtle hints, most listeners paid little attention which felt uncomfortable to him, knowing that he might have been more assertive. But telling them outright was the worst experience of all; it elicited the full range of reactions from ridicule to unwanted hero-worship. Making matters worse, his accuracy was inconsistent. Paul's most humiliating experience involved a young woman. One of his visions seemed to foretell an ominous event in her future, and he felt compelled to give her a warning. She accepted his prediction at face value and took precautionary measures. When the event didn't happen, she became angry, berating him as a fraud and chiding him for unduly frightening her. Obviously, this was upsetting, and he really wanted nothing more than to be finished with the whole unreliable phenomenon.

We decided to try an experiment. Paul explained that he could usually tell when one of his sleeping dreams was of the prophetic kind. These tended to be vivid; the colors in the dream scenes were particularly bright. I asked him to get in touch with me immediately whenever he had such a dream, even if he was awakened by it in the middle of the night. I suggested that we go through the symbols together, analyzing them, using the five-step technique. He agreed, and during our subsequent phone conversations we worked our way through his dreams, treating each part symbolically, remembering that the intended recipient of the message was himself.

The results of our experiment were thought provoking. Despite his prior pattern, none of these particular instances "came true." Each dream happened only once—during sleep. We were intrigued and heartened by this change, but realized that it would take much more data to hypothesize an explanation or general rule. Nevertheless, the results seemed to imply that at least one important purpose of Paul's prophetic dreams was to deliver a message to himself.

After a few of these sessions, our paths didn't cross until several months later. When they did, he explained that the prophetic phenomenon had ceased altogether. He actually felt a sense of guilt about it, fearing that "the universe" had given him a gift which he had simply squandered. I asked him how he was feeling. He told me that life was much calmer for him these days. He had also gotten the gist of the dream technique and had begun looking at his "normal" dreams in the same light, from time to time gaining a helpful insight. I asked him if he thought this new sense of peace and these dream insights were any less a gift from the universe than what he had been experiencing so distressingly before.

46

Dean Radin and scientific evidence support the existence of paranormal phenomena.

From the perspective of a "normal" view of life, prophecy is one of those phenomena that is not supposed to happen; no one ought to be able to predict the future based purely on some nebulous inner "knowing." Yet there are those who do. There is also credible evidence that some people have other types of strange experiences that ought to be impossible. For example, there are individuals who purport to have clairvoyant skills. Others remember past lives. Still others see what they think are ghosts.

Skeptics tend to lump all of these experiences into the realm of the paranormal and dismiss them out of hand. Yet all these experiences, however strange, are relevant to the waking dream: Whatever you perceive, is you. This is as true for “weird” experiences as it is for the most ordinary occurrences in daily life. In the next few chapters, we will take a brief look at such events. But because paranormal phenomena elicit such a wide variety of reactions, it will be helpful to first establish a basis of objective understanding.

Possibly the single most convincing research being done to validate paranormal phenomena is the work of physicist and author, Dean Radin. His book, *The Conscious Universe—the Scientific Truth of Psychic Phenomena*, represents a milestone in the field. A former member of the Princeton University physics faculty, Radin's credentials are impeccable. His research is exhaustive, and the conclusion he reaches—namely, that the validity of psychic phenomena has already been established beyond any reasonable doubt—is difficult to refute. Laying out a convincing argument, he cites study after carefully executed study. Often the results of these research projects were immediately refuted by skeptics in the scientific community who claimed that the methods employed were flawed. In several of these disputed cases, the researchers themselves went to the skeptics for advice. They asked these doubters for a set of criteria which they could establish in order to render the study valid. In a few such instances, the skeptics followed through; the study was repeated using the new criteria, and still the results were significant.[28]

Radin would wholeheartedly agree that there is an important link between our inner and outer worlds, although he would use other terminology. His research convincingly demonstrates that people can see, experience and "know" things that, according to the generally accepted view of life, are impossible. For our purposes, this validation is helpful because paranormal and psychic phenomena are an intrinsic part of the waking dream. If you perceive it, it is because it is a reflection of your current state of awareness, and you have brought the perception into your life in order to grow.

---

[28] Radin, Dean; The Conscious Universe; p. 43, p. 55, pp. 87-89.

47

The paranormal and unresolved issues are understood as unfinished business.

Radin's research into psychic phenomena represents the approach most rooted in the scientific method. But there are other approaches to the paranormal as well. In the 1960s, Indian yogi, Swami Rama Bharati, allowed himself to be studied by scientists at the Menninger Clinic. Using his mind, Bharati successfully controlled various autonomic bodily processes, such as heart rate, blood pressure and body temperature.[29] Until then, doing so was thought to be impossible. His success was viewed as a breakthrough by the Menninger Clinic; they saw it as evidence legitimizing a human's ability to use his mind for purposes much more sophisticated than thinking.

Others have pointed to the limitations of our scientific knowledge when it comes to understanding strange events that don't seem to follow accepted scientific principles. Hungarian physicist and scientific philosopher, Ervin Laszlo, wrote extensively on the anomalies in our current scientific models. He pointed out that there are many ways in which these models do not describe what actually occurs in life. He then went on to theorize that a satisfactory understanding of occurrences that do not "follow the rules" will only come after a more careful study of inner, mystical practices.[30] According to him, until there is a greater acceptance of a blend between our inner and our outer experiences, our models will continue to be inaccurate.

At the other end of the paranormal research spectrum are members of the "Paranormal Research Society" at Pennsylvania State University. In this organization, intelligent, non-superstitious and admirably educated individuals study the craft and science of demonology.[31] Among other activities, these students respond to the distress calls of people plagued by intruding spirits. Using techniques, some of which are reminiscent of a *Dracula* movie, they actually perform exorcisms. To them there is no question about another realm

---

[29] Tigunait, Pandit Rajmain; At the Eleventh Hour; pp. 145-148.

[30] Laszlo, Ervin; Science and the Akashic Field; pp. 24-58.

[31] paranormalresearchsociety.org/overview-history/

that influences this one (and vice-versa), sometimes in an unsavory manner.

There are many ways of understanding the paranormal, and ghosts in particular, but for the purposes of the waking dream, the Sufi healer and luminary, Reshad Feild, offers the clearest and simplest explanation. He says, simply, "Ghosts are unfinished business." Unfinished business. Like so many simple and deceptively off-hand remarks, it took me years to understand what he meant by this. When I finally did, I realized that his approach to the paranormal is the one most closely aligned to the discussion in this book.

When speaking of the waking dream, it is important to remember that whatever you perceive, is you. As has been argued throughout, on some subliminal level we seem to participate in the creation of our own waking dream reality, filling our lives with external images—everything from Stan's Dobermans to Tim's seagulls on the Malibu beach to Austin's cruise control. No matter how diverse they are, these images are all metaphors for the issues we are grappling with. This is true for anything coming into our awareness, including ghosts. In an odd twist, those who are skeptical of the paranormal are correct. They are likely to argue that these phenomena are "made up," and they have a point: from the perspective of the waking dream, all of us "make up" everything we perceive.

Many important dream messages—waking or sleeping—come in a jolting manner. In the last chapters it was shown that sometimes they can be downright unpleasant while they work overtime to grab our groggy attention. Eunice's awareness was captured by an over-sexed husband during her waking hours. The climber had a near-miss with a large rock while he was asleep. Jung, as a child, was shocked by the vision of a turd falling on a cathedral. The young man named Paul with inaccurate prophetic dreams had to be humiliated before he finally turned the attention of his unusual visions on himself. In each case the same pattern unfolded: an unpleasant perception led to a sense of bewilderment. That evolved into a desire for an explanation, and ultimately, the solution came when the dreamer looked to himself for an answer. Before that, the dreamer was struggling with an issue that had yet to be resolved: unfinished business.

All of the dreams just mentioned were unsettling and captured the dreamer's attention. In that respect, they were the same. But in every other way, they were as varied as life itself. There was a vision, there was a runaway boulder, there was sex, and there was prophecy. There were invasive seagulls, there were Dobermans, there was a cruise control. Elsewhere in this book there have been divorces, paintings, obnoxious restaurant employees, cars in the shape of human brains, and bars of soap. To that collection—which could be expanded *ad infinitim*—one can easily add paranormal phenomena.

When viewed from the perspective of the dream, these experiences are the same. Every one of them represents a struggle that the dreamer has yet to put to rest. In other words, they are the dreamer's unfinished business.

48

The paranormal is viewed as a dream: ghosts and past lives.

From the perspective of the dream, a paranormal experience is simply another form of an unusual occurrence offered as a metaphor for one's growth. For that reason, let's continue to explore these kinds of events.

These days, on certain television channels, one can view programs about ghosts and peoples' efforts to rid themselves of these intruders. Someone in this predicament might well disagree with the idea that they have subliminally participated in the process, that they were part of what caused such apparitions to come into their lives as waking dream symbols: "No, you're wrong! I did not 'manifest' these things as you imply. It turned out that our house was built right on top of a Civil War cemetery. These spirits were real."

Bizarre phenomena happen all the time, and perhaps the above claims are true. My only response would come in the form of a question: Of the tens of thousands of homes that are bought and sold on a regular basis in the United States, what was it that attracted you to a house built on a forgotten graveyard? Perhaps it was something as innocent and simple as the appealing slope of the lawn. Maybe it was more substantive, like the layout of the rooms or the convenience of a nearby grocery store or a highly-touted school system. Maybe the taxes were low, or your best friend lived nearby, or the price was attractive.

And possibly, there was something else at work as well. Why do any of us make the choices we do? In the seemingly-random nature of life, why do some of the things we decide to do turn out well? Then other choices, with just as much potential—like attractive houses—become disappointments or problems. I submit that we bring these problems into our lives in order to provide us with metaphors that can help us resolve personal issues.

Consider another extreme type of paranormal occurrence: Do you, or someone you know, have a particularly vivid past life recollection? This is not uncommon. People under hypnosis have been recorded speaking languages they do not know, relating details of lives from another time period about which they are completely ignorant.[32] These kinds of "recollections" can inspire wonder. Yet, for a moment, try to separate yourself from this sense of awe, and like the climber who was nearly hit by a falling boulder, make an effort to understand the phenomenon from a different perspective. For starters, if a person remembers one past life, then presumably there have been others. What was it about this particular memory that brought it so poignantly back into the present? It would be interesting to treat it as a dream. If whatever you perceive, is you, then it has come to a person's attention because it represents something currently being worked on—unfinished business.

In this book so far, there have been over a dozen dream scenarios presented, from both sleep and wakefulness. These experiences have had the following in common: In each case, the person was bothered by the event; it became an abrasion in his life. Then, the solution came not from an external rescuer, but from the dreamer, himself, taking ownership of the conflict. This has been no different whether the experience was something "normal"—like divorces—or "bizarre"—like a prophetic dream that comes true. The symbols from both the bizarre and normal events served the same purpose: to alert the dreamer to personal issues that needed resolution. The symbolic images came into the dreamer's life for the same reason that all dream symbols come to us: to deliver a message of instruction and guidance.

[32] Stevenson, Ian; Unlearned Language; pp. 157-161. 127.

49

Logical and illogical life events are examined side by side.

The last chapters have discussed some paranormal occurrences, including ghosts, haunted graveyards and individuals prophesying the future. Most of us don't have such unusual experiences, nevertheless we participate in a blend of two different kinds of life events. One I will call logical events, the other illogical events.

Logical events: These are experiences we have where there is a clear cause and effect. We overtly create the cause and can definitely witness all facets of the effect: John picks up a dinner plate that he doesn't realize is hot. In his surprise and discomfort, he lets go of it immediately and it falls back onto the kitchen counter with a loud clatter. This is a prime example of an overt stimulus resulting in a predictable response. It can be witnessed and logically analyzed by anyone viewing it. Most likely, everyone watching will pretty much see the same thing. In that sense John's experience with the plate is visible; it is a logical, objective experience.

Illogical events: These are incidents that occur in our lives in which we experience an effect, however we do not overtly cause it. There is no visible outer logic, and therefore the event cannot easily be observed, explained or analyzed. The outcome is unpredictable.

An example: A contented woman's life radically changes when she finds herself a witness to a crime. The legal process is long and involved, and it drains enormous amounts of her time and energy.

In this illogical instance, the woman who has been impacted has done nothing overtly to bring the change into her life; there is no direct cause and effect. It's as if life itself simply decided to play a nasty trick, and the affected woman suddenly has to face an entirely new set of circumstances without having done anything to bring it about.

Why do these things take place? What causes their specific timing? Who dictates that they will happen to Person A and not to Person B? The easiest answer to those questions is to say that these events are random; they are simply among life's unfair and unpredictable misadventures that we are all subjected to from time to time.

However, I offer another way of looking at them. If one goes through the five simple steps of analyzing such illogical occurrences as waking dreams, one might be surprised to see that there is, in fact, a logical cause and effect. The difficulty is that we cannot witness the whole sequence of events. Unlike John's mishap with the hot dinner plate—an incident that we can all watch—much of the buildup to these other types of illogical-seeming misfortunes happens invisibly in an inner realm. I am arguing that the seemingly-arbitrary unfairness that suddenly manifested in the life of the crime witness was deliberate. Further, the "victim" was subliminally, subconsciously involved in bringing this injustice into her life. But since the unconscious decision was made in a realm that couldn't be observed, it seemed capricious and unfair.

The above example was hypothetical. Let's now take an actual incident and use the five steps of dream interpretation to examine the unfortunate experience of a teacher named Sarah. Her world was suddenly thrown into turmoil when life dealt her an unexpected blow. Rather than deciding that her experience was a random, illogical event perpetrated on her by the injustice of the universe, we'll treat her misfortune as a waking dream. Here is the analysis of her dream in its entirety:

Step 1: Relate the dream.

Sarah is a gifted educator of children who has an aversion to self-promotion. Budget cutbacks in her school district resulted in the loss of her job. Instead of going through the process of writing up her impressive résumé and actively seeking another position, she took an available position as the caretaker for an elderly woman. This choice resulted in a pay cut, but she found this option easier than having to promote herself as she looked for openings in the teaching profession. The elderly woman was healthy, and Sarah seemed to have found a solution to her employment problem that would keep her working for the foreseeable future, even though she was not using her excellent teaching skills.

But one day the elderly woman fell and broke her hip. She was hospitalized and subsequently moved to an assisted-living facility. Overnight, Sarah was unemployed, finding herself in an economic panic because the event was unexpected; she had done nothing to cause the end of her job; it simply vanished.

Step 2: Isolate the symbols.

teaching children

losing your job

schools

elderly woman

giving care

falling and breaking a hip

Step 3: Interpret the symbols as metaphors.

David: Tell me about teaching.

Sarah: It's the job I do best. I'm good at explaining things, and I love to watch a face light up when a child understands a new idea.

David: Tell me about children or, as you just said, "a child."

Sarah: A child is a youngster, a person who hasn't reached maturity.

David: Tell me about losing your job.

Sarah: There were budget cutbacks, not enough resources. The school couldn't afford to keep me any longer, and it took my work away.

David: Tell me about schools.

Sarah: They are places where you go to learn.

David: Tell me about an elderly woman.

Sarah: This one is certainly a nice person, but she doesn't have much more time in this life. She has probably done just about all of the important things she is going to do.

David: Tell me about giving care to an elderly woman.

Sarah: My caretaking job didn't really require any great skill. This lady was living independently, but she was getting forgetful, and there were certain things that she could no longer do for herself. I was there mostly to help make sure her life ran smoothly.

David: Tell me about falling and breaking a hip.

Sarah: For her, it signaled the end of her life as she had been living it. For me, it was scary because it meant that my job came to an abrupt end and, frankly, I'm not sure what to do next.

Step 4: Retell the dream, using and owning the metaphors.

David: Sarah, if this dream were mine, I'd say that there is a part of me that has a job. The job takes place in the area inside myself where I go to learn things. And my job is explaining things to the parts of myself that haven't yet reached maturity. I love doing this because it's what I do best, and I enjoy seeing my own face light up when I understand something new.

But suddenly I have taken this job away from myself because I don't have the necessary resources to keep it going. Instead, I find myself working with another part of me. It's a part that is nice but which doesn't have much more time left in my life. It has probably done all the important things it's going to do. This new job really doesn't take much skill. Mostly, I am here to make sure things run smoothly because this part of me is getting forgetful and can't quite do everything for itself anymore. Then, suddenly, the life of this older part of me comes to an end, and I am out of a job again. I don't know where to go. It's scary.

Step 5: Explore the dream's relevance in your life.

In our subsequent conversation we talked about the two types of jobs she had given herself. One type was with the younger parts of herself, parts that had not yet reached maturity and were hungry for new ideas. The other job was with an older part of herself, a part that was nearing its end in her life. I asked her if she could relate to any of this.

She immediately identified with her aversion to self-promotion. It was an "old" pattern, and she was care-taking it, nurturing it. I asked her what she thought the new, young part of her might be. She told me it had to do with breaking out of this old pattern of shying away from assertively pursuing the things she did best in life.

I asked about her comment that the job she likes to do best was taken away because of a lack of resources. Now, seeing the event as a dream, she understood that it was she who did not allocate the necessary resources. She was the one who "cut" her own "budget."

Suddenly a potential disaster in Sarah's life became an opportunity. She was giving herself a message, namely, that it was time to change an unproductive pattern that, for too long, had been part of how she faced life. It was time for her to grow, to "allocate resources" to some new patterns she needed to establish in her way of living.

As long as she tried to view her job crisis as an objective logical event—one with a tangible cause and effect, one that anyone viewing it could see and understand—it seemed random and unfair. But once she acknowledged that it came from somewhere else, somewhere that couldn't be observed so easily, from a place inside of herself—a seemingly illogical place—her crisis made sense. It was a waking dream. Once she understood it as a metaphor, she could interpret it and turn it into a positive experience. It became an opening for her to pursue a new, more constructive way of living her life.

50

Logical and illogical events work in conjunction with each other.

Most of us do not see the illogical-seeming incidents in our lives as occurring in any sort of predictable pattern. But when we do, we learn that there is a deliberate and calculated connection between logical and illogical occurrences.

By way of a hypothetical example, let's imagine someone in a state of personal crisis. We'll call him Matthew. Because of his preoccupation with an overwhelming issue, important details of Matthew's life are ignored. He forgets to pay his bills; eventually, the power company cuts off his electricity. When he realizes that he can't turn on his lights, he is distraught and grabs the keys to his car so he can get out of the house for a while. He puts them into the ignition, tries to start his sedan, but nothing happens. In his distress, Matthew bangs his head against the steering wheel and says, "I can already tell: this is going to be one of those days."

The first of Matthew's calamities was the result of a logical sequence of events: He was distracted by his personal crisis and didn't pay a bill; then the electric company discontinued his service. For the second, there was no obvious cause and effect; why should his car suddenly not run?

Now let's step back for a moment and look at both of these events from the perspective of the waking dream and metaphor: Matthew is in crisis, and his "power has been turned off." What's more, "his vehicle won't start; it doesn't work." Both of the annoyances he experienced—one predictable, the other random-seeming—are describing his own state of affairs to him. In fact, both waking dreams are trying desperately to deliver the same message. The two communications—"power has been turned off" and "the engine is malfunctioning"—are telling him: "Your internal system is breaking down and you need to give it your full attention."

The trouble is that it is so easy for him to see the logical events in his life as self-contained—complete in themselves. "Oh well, I didn't pay my bill. It makes perfect sense that my electricity was turned off. I guess I'd better write a check to the power company." And that's where his analysis of the situation ends. Then, when he experiences an event that seems to occur with no sense of logical sequence, he rationalizes it away. "Isn't that typical of life? Just when you're trying to deal with your power going out, your car won't start. What a hassle!" We can all identify with his behavior.

In general, when we begin to make a metaphoric connection, seeing both logical and illogical events in our lives as similar types of communications, we start to observe the way the two varieties of experiences work in conjunction with each other. In Matthew's case, he had a pair of back-to-back events, one with an observable progression of consequences, the other random-seeming, and he interpreted them as life ganging up on him, which was not the case at all.

When we finally recognize the events of our lives as metaphors, we learn that the appearances of both logical and illogical situations are not only orchestrated but are often designed to come into our awareness simultaneously, delivering a message that is twice as strong as it might have been had only one incident made an appearance. Further, we begin to understand that, working together, they weave our outer lives into a kind of surreal tapestry that is, well . . .dreamlike.

51

It is possible to juggle the paradox of two different views of the world.

The majority of us try to live our lives in as conventional a fashion as we can. We shop for groceries, take our kids to school, care for our elders, and in general, attend to the affairs of our mundane lives. Yet throughout this book, and especially in the last few chapters, I have suggested a radically different way of looking at our world, one that is all about metaphors and a dreamlike quality to our experiences. I have proposed that what we see presented to us in our lives is based on our own thought patterns, and sometimes in a crisis, our need to grow out of those patterns. I have used phrases like the inner and the outer, the subjective and the objective, the logical and the illogical and the normal and the paranormal. In fact, what I have presented is a model of life that is a paradox. It confronts us with two vastly different views of the world, each one demanding that we approach life in a way that seems irreconcilable with its philosophical counterpart. How do we juggle this?

There are three ways to deal with this paradox: One can ignore the waking dream concept, one can become obsessed with it, or one can balance these two extremes. Let's examine the options.

The more common approach to the paradox is simply not to acknowledge the waking dream metaphor at all. When we experience events in our lives that are shocking, bizarre or repetitive, we take them at face value rather than seeing them as dream metaphors. Thus they take us by surprise and cause distress. Recall Matthew in Chapter 50 whose electricity went out and whose car wouldn't run; like him, we might end up (figuratively) banging our heads against a steering wheel.

At the other end of the spectrum are those who try to live their lives exclusively from the perspective of a dream metaphor. That way of living presents its own problems. When all you are doing is viewing life as a metaphor, it's pretty hard to deal with the day-to-day affairs of the world like cleaning your house or showing up for work on time.

Consider the following example of being overly influenced by dream metaphors: Back in the 1970s when such "new age" attitudes were popular, a woman at a dream workshop actually announced that she had deliberately distanced herself from her children's issues. This was because she now understood that they created their own realities, and it was up to them to manage what they manifested—problems and all; she need have no part of it. When she made her views known, she was informed in no uncertain terms that she was mistaken, that she had made her decision based on a half-truth. While it might be correct that her children would one day recognize their own participation in creating their realities through the waking dream metaphor, they were not ready to do so, not until they were nurtured to maturity. As I recall, I used the image of a baby eagle whose destiny it is to soar high above the earth. But if its mother pushes it out of the nest before it has feathers, it will simply plummet to the ground and perish.

We have discussed two extreme approaches to handling the paradox of logical and illogical, objective and subjective experiences. Is there a middle ground to juggling these two conflicting life views?

Tenzin Wangyal Rinpoche, a Tibetan lama of the Bön tradition who has spent much time exploring these relationships puts it this way:

It is important to take care of responsibilities and to respect the logic and limitations of conventional life. When you tell yourself that your waking life is a dream, this is true, but if you leap from a building you will still fall, not fly. If you do not go to work, bills will go unpaid. Plunge your hand in a fire and you will be burned. It is important to remain grounded in the realities of the relative world, because as long as there is a "you" and "me" there is a relative world in which we live, other sentient beings who are suffering, and consequences from the decisions we make.[33]

That is excellent advice; it acknowledges the importance of both halves of the paradox and suggests keeping a more balanced approach to living. Personally, I have found that the simplest, most stress-free way of juggling the dilemma this paradox presents us is to remember the three important dream categories: the shocking dream, the bizarre dream and the repetitive dream, first presented in Chapter 4. Like most of us, I try to live a "normal" life as much as

---

[33] Rinpoche, Tenzin Wangyal; The Tibetan Yogas of Dream and Sleep; pp. 92-93.

possible. But the minute I am confronted with a circumstance that seems alarming, peculiar or is one that just won't go away, I try to remember that I am dealing with a waking dream and its metaphoric message.

Keeping the three dream categories in the back of one's mind is a simple way to reconcile these two seemingly-incompatible world views. However, it requires vigilance because it is easy to slip back into the habit of viewing existence exclusively from an objective standpoint. We become like Matthew and his steering wheel in Chapter 50, seeing our calamities as misfortunes rather than as opportunities for learning through the dream metaphor. It takes work and willpower to pull oneself out of the emotional investment of a misfortune and see it from the neutral perspective of a waking dream. That is the case even for me. Remember my clash with the SUV driver in Monterey? I fumed for an entire day before it occurred to me to look at that misadventure as a dream.

Because it is so easy to slip back into life patterns that have become habitual, I find myself always pushing the philosophical limits of the dreamers I work with. My goal is to stretch them to a level of legitimate discomfort in the hope that some of what I suggest will remain in their consciousness as part of their ideology.

Think back to the rock climber featured earlier in these chapters. During sleep, he had a prophetic dream about a falling boulder; the dream then came true in his waking life. By making the suggestion that he simply had the same dream twice—once in the sleeping state and again in the awakened state—I stretched his view of the world beyond his comfort level. But even then I wasn't done with him. After he relaxed into the understanding that his sleeping and waking dreams, as seen from one level at least, were the same experience, I was able to make the following humorous admonition, although I actually did so only half in jest.

David: And by the way, if you should ever find yourself having a sleeping dream in which you see a tornado headed straight for my house? Do me a favor. Give me a call—even if it's three in the morning—so we can work through the symbols and maybe stop the whole storm right there.

What I offered him was a ludicrous suggestion—really beyond the beyond—and it was made as a lighthearted joke to break the tension in the room after I had stretched him to the point of discomfort. But now think back to the many waking dream scenarios already presented in this book; remember the changed lives of those who considered their startling waking dreams as metaphors: Ellen and Eunice worked through relationship struggles. Austin, with his cruise control, found a more satisfying work environment. The same was true after Stan encountered the Dobermans. Then there was the prophetic dreamer, Paul, who wanted nothing more than to be finished with his foretelling experiences. In his case, the action he took followed the same advice that I offered the rock climber above: understand the metaphor of a sleeping dream, and you won't have to experience it again in an awakened state.

The idea of viewing life as a metaphor is a rich, untapped realm. Any exploration of it must begin with juggling the paradox; that's the key. While living our mundane lives, going about our chores and handling our largely prosaic affairs, we can keep part of our awareness tuned to the possibility that we are also receiving dream communications from an inner, subjective, illogical-seeming source. It is one that speaks in metaphors, and often has powerful, life-altering messages to deliver.

PART EIGHT:
A MISINTERPRETED DREAM

Part Eight is a study of how a dreamer named Michael gets into trouble when he misunderstands the dream interpretation process.

52

Working on dream interpretations with another individual would have saved Michael some hardship in a love affair gone wrong.

The idea of working with someone else while interpreting dreams was first mentioned in Chapter 6. It was then reintroduced in Chapter 13 in the discussion about Ellen and her divorce ordeal. In the next few chapters, the importance of this practice will become clear. We will examine the crisis of a brilliant young man named Michael, who gets himself into humiliating trouble while trying to work on his waking dreams without the input and reflection of a trusted friend or dream facilitator.

It has been pointed out repeatedly that waking dream symbols make themselves apparent in our lives when we need a message delivered to us about personal growth. So far, less has been written about the fact that those same dream symbols change, or disappear from our lives, when the issue they are alerting us to has been resolved. That was a characteristic of the waking dream that became intriguing to Michael. He began to experiment with the idea that he could steer the direction, not only of his own life, but the life of someone else through the manipulation of dream symbols. He began, quietly, to try and engineer the nature of a love affair in an effort to alter the behavior of his fiancée. He reasoned that his fiancée, herself, was a waking dream symbol in his life. This was true. He then decided that, if he saw her exhibiting behavior that he found unsatisfactory, it was because, as a waking dream symbol in his life, she was reflecting a conflict inside of himself. This was also true.

But then he came to the conclusion that, if he changed himself, it meant that his fiancée, as a waking dream symbol, would automatically change in order to continue reflecting who he was becoming. That is where he got into trouble, because he neglected the other option: Instead of his fiancée altering her behavior like a chameleon to mirror his new persona, she might simply disappear from his life. That was what happened in Michael's case, as we will discover in detail in the next chapters.

Not only was he unsuccessful in his efforts to alter his fiancée's behavior, but his over-active mind was a disservice to him in other ways as well. Although he was successful in recognizing the metaphors in his waking life, his creative mind drew erroneous conclusions from them. He began to create a kind of fantasy around his love affair that bore little resemblance to the facts, and his whole love relationship ultimately deteriorated and fell apart.

All of this was avoidable. Had Michael been guided to work with someone else, their discussions together about dream symbols would likely have mitigated his exaggerated and inaccurate interpretations. The mere act of sharing ideas with someone else has a way of bringing those ideas into balance, and it provides a vital "reality check." Dreams are especially susceptible to wild interpretations. Think back to the early chapters of this book, the ones involving Jeremy and his dream about a mistress. Jeremy's wife, Linda, was convinced that he was having an affair, and her suspicions led to significant tensions in their marriage. Had they not sought the input of another individual, their interpretations would have remained, and their conflict might have grown. But they wisely got help, and after going through the five steps of the dream interpretation method, they came to more balanced conclusions which eventually led to the subsiding of their conflict.

Michael would have benefited in the same way had he received feedback from a friend, and had the two also gone through the five steps of the dream interpretation method. Since that didn't happen, we will use his experiences as an opportunity to learn how to avoid distressful conflicts like the one he experienced in his love relationship.

53

Michael relates the trouble he has experienced after misinterpreting a waking dream.

While on a visit to a young friend named Michael who was living in Denver, Colorado, he and I decided to take a day trip up to nearby Pike's Peak to see the spectacular views. It was April and the air was crisp. The sky was cloudless and even in chilly Denver there were signs of a spring thaw. A recent transplant to the region, Michael was eager to show me the sights.

As clear as the air was outside, at that particular moment the atmosphere in the car was clouded. Michael had something on his mind, and he was anxious to share it with me. A young and respected businessman, he was several years into a happy marriage, and was recently accepted as a member of MENSA International, also known as the society of geniuses. He had much going for him, but he was troubled at the moment, still nursing the wounds of an old love affair gone sour, one in which he was the inadvertent cause of its demise.

In high school Michael had been active in an innovative and effective peer counseling program where he was trained to constructively intervene when he recognized schoolmates in serious emotional distress. So the fact that he later deceived and deeply hurt his then-fiancée, still weighed heavily on his conscience. The reason I was privy to this distress was that his failed love was due to a long-term manipulation on his part, one that was based on the principles of the waking dream. It was I who had taught him the concepts and showed him the subtleties of the dream's "magic."

Having known Michael most of his life, I excitedly explained the dream concepts to him when he was still a youngster. This was a time when they were new to me as well. His quick mind and easy grasp of these ideas were intoxicating, and I did not temper my enthusiasm with a comparable dose of caution; back then, I didn't know that I needed to. Michael grew up with a sense of being empowered by this "secret" and allowed himself to be seduced into thinking he could manipulate his life, almost like a super-hero.

In his present outpouring to me, he wanted clarification of what went wrong. Further, he was determined to point out the flaws of a technique and system that had let him down profoundly. He explained, “The problem is that, when I recognize a waking dream in my life, I can make it mean anything I want it to. My mind has a field day, steering me down all kinds of bogus little pathways." Even after all this time Michael’s pain and confusion were palpable, and I found myself pensive and remorseful.

When he met his ex-fiancée, Renée, he recognized immediately that there would be issues in the relationship, but the attraction was strong, the affection sincere, and he was determined to overcome any difficulties. For him it became a rescue mission. He decided to use the dream as one of his primary tools, unfortunately, without the benefit of a system of checks and balances. His remark to me was an obvious indicator that I had given him only enough information to be dangerous to himself: “I can make a waking dream mean anything I want it to.” Absolutely true. Which is why, when analyzing a dream, a great deal of emphasis is now placed on working with someone else and going meticulously through each step of the interpretation process.

Michael didn’t do that. He easily recognized waking dreams as they arose in his life; he was good at that. But when he saw the significance of one—especially one that was relevant to his relationship—he made no attempt to test his own perceptions against those of someone else. He simply made note of it internally and gave his fiercely intelligent mind free reign to reach any conclusions it devised. He didn’t even go through a silent "Tell me about it!" question-and-answer process. Over time, he developed a kind of fantasy about the direction his love relationship was headed, one that had less and less to do with what was actually going on.

He got himself into trouble in another way as well. He assumed that his waking dream symbols would remain in his life, simply changing if he changed. He ignored the possibility that, alternatively, they might disappear altogether. This was his reasoning:

If whatever I perceive, is me, then it stands to reason that Renée is a reflection of who I am. This means that, if there are problems in our relationship, those problems are ones I am dealing with inside myself as well. So, if I study those relationship conflicts carefully, I can use them to help me change myself.

So far so good, but now it went off the deep end:

Therefore, if I change myself, it stands to reason that Renée will change, too, to reflect who I have now become. In this manner I can quietly, subtly alter her personality by helping her grow as a person while maneuvering our relationship into a more acceptable and functional one.

As well-intentioned as Michael's scheme was, it also represented an effort on his part to be omnipotent and to force change in an individual who may or may not have been ready for it—or even interested in it. Michael did make shifts in his life, consciously using the dream to make successful changes in himself, however Renée continued her existence more or less as she always had. The net result was an increase in their differences and viewpoints, exactly the opposite effect than intended.

The result was detrimental to them both. During his initial belief in the process and while still confident of his success, he had made marriage commitments to Renée, further enmeshing their lives until he realized that his plan was backfiring. Then, in an abrupt and unexpected announcement, he felt obliged to renege on his promises, bringing anguish to each of them. In addition to the predictable trauma of a romantic breakup, Michael was dealing with his own shame, embarrassment and loss of pride. A skilled counselor, he had mistakenly allowed himself to experiment well past the bounds of appropriate conduct, and he had paid a steep price.

The car trip up to Pike's Peak was our first opportunity to revisit these old events with their implications and to bring closure to them. Michael was anxious to impress upon me the potential shortcomings of depending on the dream for anything substantive. In his thoughtful and measured comments, he implied that the dream, if used for important matters, was comparable to a hoax; he saw that his reliance on it had gotten him into serious trouble.

In my own quiet sadness at having been an unwitting contributor to his pain, it did not seem appropriate for me to point out that, in fact, Michael's dream worked perfectly. Whatever you perceive, is you. As we have witnessed so often throughout this book, you attract what metaphorically reflects your state of mind. Michael and Renée were drawn to each other because they symbolically represented important aspects of each other. By the same token, when Michael began to change, their symbolic representation of each other was no longer valid. He was becoming someone else, and Renée stopped accurately reflecting him.

It would take several years before Michael would understand the dynamics of this process and his participation in it. These days, he takes responsibility for his actions. At the time, what he experienced was an unpleasant shock when he discovered that he was unable to play God and manipulate the nature of the outcome, especially when his maneuvering represented a conscious effort to affect the life of another individual. Ultimately, Michael and Renée's parting was appropriate, because what Michael was trying to do represented a form of mind control.

These understandings, when they eventually came to him, would be brand new ideas. In the meantime he and I had more to discuss on our trip up to Pike's Peak.

54

Michael attempted to change his fiancée by manipulating a waking dream, but he was unsuccessful.

One of the things that got Michael into so much trouble was trying to engineer the direction and course of a waking dream scenario. His reasoning was that, if he altered his attitudes, his fiancée would also change to reflect who he had become. She was, after all, his waking dream symbol. He correctly perceived potential problems in their relationship, and thought that if he made constructive shifts in his approach to life, it would result in comparable growth in Renée.

It was an admirable scheme, but it was doomed to failure. In the hundreds of dreams I have listened to and worked with, I have witnessed profound changes, always reflecting an inner attitude shift on the dreamer's part. Since those with whom I work tend to be looking for solutions to conflicts in their own lives, these changes, for the most part, bring relief. But never once have I known of someone who could actually dictate the exact nature of a dream's resolution for someone else; the dream is a purely personal affair.

As Michael discovered, life can be complicated. As has been suggested, it is both a metaphoric and an objective experience. Our sense of stability comes from the objective part. That part helps us bond to others, offers us a sense of continuity and a much needed perception of logical cause and effect. Yet even the most stable, long-term symbols in our lives—our families, our marriages, our nationalities, our occupations, our neighborhoods—are waking dream metaphors. As such they are subject to the same behavior that all dream symbols exhibit: They come into our awareness when they reflect who we are. However, if we change and they no longer metaphorically depict us, they disappear from our consciousness. Think of Ellen's husband who receded from her life as she was experiencing profound growth within herself. Then there was Austin and his cruise control. After he did some important work on his attitudes, his career fell apart only to be replaced by something that better reflected who he had become.

The same was true for Michael and Renée. They were together because they metaphorically reflected important qualities in each other. When Michael began to change, it altered the dynamic between them. His altered persona left the two of them with a metaphoric ultimatum: Something else would have to occur if they were to continue as waking dream symbols for each other. For example, Michael could abandon his efforts at self-improvement and go back to the way he had been before. These two would then reflect each other, metaphorically, once again. But that was unlikely. As another option, Renée could follow Michael on his quest for self-improvement, making her own attitude shifts. In that way, the metaphoric dynamic between them would remain valid, with both of them walking a parallel path of growth. That kind of thing often happens in close relationships; both individuals change, and as long as they continue to reflect each other metaphorically, they stay together.

However, Michael continued on his new course of change, but Renée remained the same. As a result, Michael's effort to manipulate her so that the two of them could stay together was a failure. The predictable outcome of their crisis was a separation because they ceased to act as waking dream metaphors for each other. Such separations are also common in life; couples part ways all the time.

In Michael's case it was just as well because, through his scheme, he was actually trying to control Renée subliminally. It didn't work. Instead, what he eventually learned was that the only thing he had control over was himself. Everything else in his life—including his fiancée—was a waking dream metaphor that, when it ceased to reflect who he had become, disappeared.

Those realizations would take time. For the moment, Michael and I were riding in his car, wending our way up a mountain and still wrestling with the validity of the waking dream in general. Each of us was articulate and respectful as we intensely tried to get our points across to the other, but neither of us accomplished more than being listened to.

Well into our drive, we rounded a curve on the winding road up this dramatic mountain and found ourselves face to face with a National Park Service barrier which prevented further travel. The attached sign explained that, due to heavy snow accumulation in the higher elevations, the road was closed from here on. Michael, perhaps in some frustration at how our morning had been transpiring, turned to me and wanted to know, "What does your waking dream have to say about this?"

I answered, "It seems to be telling us that you and I have been on a trip to view our world from the highest possible vantage point. Then, along the way, we came to a road block. It's obvious that the avenue is there. It's just that, at the moment, it's frozen solid."

So even in the midst of our passionate discussion, part of which was an attempt to invalidate the waking dream, the dream, itself, was making its presence felt. It was doing what waking dreams do best during intense moments in our lives, namely, providing us with dramatic symbolic imagery of our states of mind. It was telling us that we were not in a position to proceed.

Since the road was closed, Michael quietly turned the car around. Our conversation first lagged, then moved on to more mundane topics, neither of us wanting to jeopardize the friendship.

It would be years before we were able to broach the waking dream topic again with each other. When we did, we both had the advantage of intervening life. In addition, the pain of Michael's romantic breakup had long since receded. Now we were able to hear each other's concerns, with Michael taking responsibility for his attempted manipulation of Renée. At the same time, I was able to point out safeguards that I had put in place in the dream-analysis process—an emphasis on working with someone else and on proceeding methodically through the five steps of symbol interpretation. As he and I talked, occasionally shaking our heads at the twists and turns of life's journey, it quietly occurred to me that, had we now been in Denver, we would have made it up to Pike's Peak.

55

Michael learned the importance of caution in dream analysis.

The more dreams I have observed and helped interpret, the more cautious I have become. As with all tools, the process can be beneficial in the right context but counterproductive in the wrong one. It took Michael years to grow past his pain. For a long time the dream represented no more than chicanery to him. Only now, many years later, will he even entertain the possibility of its validity.

Fortunately, Michael's case is an exception; the majority of dreamers have constructive, helpful experiences. That is largely due to a set of protocols that, gradually, have been put into place over the years, guidelines designed to help avoid the kind of distress Michael experienced. Most of them have already been discussed, but there are a few details that need highlighting.

Therefore, the ensuing chapters will review the whole interpretation process step by step, filling in those few gaps that were left implicit, including both the techniques and their inherent pitfalls.

PART NINE: STEP BY STEP

Part Nine presents a methodical review of dream interpretation techniques, including some common pitfalls.

56

Dream interpretation techniques: Communicating with metaphors, puns and word-plays—a common communication device, both in and out of dreams.

The dream language of metaphors was discussed in detail for the first time in Chapter 10. The purpose of this chapter is to expand that discussion. It is true that dreams communicate primarily in metaphors. However, on occasion they make use of other types of word-plays as well. Puns and double entendre—where one meaning of a word or image is obvious but a second one is partially obscured and has to be revealed—are both devices that are employed from time to time. Occasionally, the word-plays in these dreams provide relief from the more serious dream events that most of us experience; dreams can demonstrate a surprising sense of humor.

One of my favorite examples of a word-play during a sleeping dream is the case of a serious young man named Martin. He was searching for his life's direction. He had been an athlete all through high school and college; that had been his passion, and he hadn't thought about much else. Now, in his thirties, he was the father of a growing family, and he wanted to explore something that was more in-depth; he wanted to provide himself, his wife and his children with a greater variety of life's offerings. His search had taken on the quality of a seeker looking for a guru on a mountain top; it was impassioned and intense. He had joined a dream class I was teaching in southern California because his nearly-obsessive quest had begun to invade the images of his sleep, and he thought that the answers might come from his dreams. One evening during class he related the following sleeping dream.

Martin: In my dream I'm up in the air, flying around, searching for the answers to all these questions that have been on my mind for so long. As I look around from up there, I realize I'm somewhere I've never been before. I try to identify it, and I think to myself that I must be in some place like Louisiana, because I'm flying over a bayou. And that's all I can remember.

Having spent so many years studying the language of dreams, I began to smile right away and took the liberty of helping Martin interpret this dream by myself, not waiting for the rest of the class to catch on to the dream's word-play joke. I began grilling Martin relentlessly, the whole time with a big grin on my face.

David: So, Martin, you're looking for answers to your most pressing life questions and you're where?

Martin: The nearest I can tell is that I seem to be in Louisiana, because I'm flying over a bayou.

David: You're looking for answers to your most pressing questions and you're in Louisiana flying over..?

Martin: [perplexed at my repetition] I said I'm flying over a bayou.

David: You're looking for answers to your most pressing questions and you're flying over...?

Martin: [frustrated and raising his voice] a bayou.

David: You're looking for answers to your most pressing questions and you're flying over a...?

Martin: [clearly annoyed] BAYOU!

At that point, most of the class—including Martin—got the joke and started laughing. Martin's dream was a humorous admonition, not only advising him to lighten up, but directly addressing his pressing concern. It was telling him, "Martin, you don't have to search in places that are alien to you—like Louisiana; you can stay home. What you are looking for is by you." He was being admonished to spend some quiet time with his own thoughts; that is where he would find the answers to his questions.

The laughter in the class eventually died down. What remained for the rest of the evening was the look of wonder on Martin's face. He had been delivered a message that was both humorous and succinct, and he was amazed that something so witty, poignant and helpful had come from his own imagination. It was a life-changing moment for him, not only addressing his pressing concern, but doing so using a unique and delightful "language," a word-play involving a double meaning. In fact, as the class cheerfully pondered the "bayou" imagery in Martin's dream, members realized that it could be interpreted in another sense as well: "buy you." While everyone present admitted that this meaning was more obscure, the idea of Martin "purchasing," or more generally, "acquiring" answers to his questions was part of the overall theme.

As stated in Chapter 10, we communicate this way in our dreams, but we also use images in conversation on a daily basis: "She was the apple of his eye." She was the apple of his eye? What does that mean? Taken literally, it's nonsense; only as a word-play—in this case, a metaphor—does it have the meaning of a special fondness for someone. And yet, like Martin's dream of strangely flying over a Louisiana swamp, it is easy to imagine a woman excitedly walking into a dream class reporting that she'd had a sleeping dream in which her lover had looked at her longingly, but had done so through eyes that were really apples. That is how dreams "talk to us." And implicit in this example is the understanding that dreams use a language of imagery that is similar to a language we use in our daily communications.

I decided to find out how common such metaphoric expressions are in our ordinary speech and began haphazardly collecting examples of the ones we use. I was surprised. I had expected to record perhaps a dozen, maybe even twenty. Yet, with little effort, over a period of a few weeks, I compiled the long list of sayings that comprises Appendix C. There are well over 600 examples, and I am confident that, were I to put in a truly conscientious effort, I could have found many more.

"She was the apple of his eye." "He lost his head." "They rubbed salt in his wounds." "Her mood was black." "That kid is a monster!" "I stepped into my boss's shoes." These are all common remarks used in daily speech. And yet any one of them, taken literally, is absurd. Like the language of dreams, they are metaphoric images which we use on a regular basis as we casually converse with each other. This kind of visual imagery—whether in dreams or out of them—seems to be an intrinsic part of our communication process.

The only difference between the metaphoric imagery we use when we are talking to each other and that of our dreams is that, when we say these things, we put less attention on the visual aspects being described. Because of this, the imagery recedes from prominence. In a dream—either a sleeping dream or a waking dream—if the expression "I stepped into my boss's shoes" were to become relevant, we would likely find ourselves literally walking around in a pair of highly polished dress shoes that belonged to our employer.

This illustrates that the dream language of imagery through puns, word-plays and metaphors is not alien to us. Learning to be consciously aware of this mode of language is the first prerequisite to working with dreams. I spend a great deal of time in dream classes gently steering dreamers away from taking dream images literally; dreams speak to us in the language of images, and dreamers need to become fluently aware of that language.

57

Dream interpretation techniques: Recognizing the symbols.

Many people, when confronted with a poignant dream, aren't sure what to do with it. Where should they begin? How should they approach something as illogical as the plot of a bizarre sleeping dream? Is it appropriate to take a crisis in waking life and treat it as a waking dream, a metaphor?

Probably the biggest stumbling block to interpreting a dream is that one has to begin by facing an inexplicable jumble of symbols. The symbols are usually more perplexing when the dream is a sleeping dream, but they can be enigmatic in a waking dream as well, especially when the dreamer is emotionally invested in the experience. It is often difficult to step back and look at the symbols impartially. While the interpretation of dreams involves a simple enough technique, knowing exactly what to look for and how to assemble the various clues into a cohesive story takes practice, patience and self-discipline. It is all too easy to become discouraged, throwing one's hands into the air in a gesture of defeat, or worse, taking a poorly thought-out stab at defining the metaphoric images one identifies.

One of the best ways to become adept at recognizing the significant symbols in a dream is to keep a journal. Simply write the dreams down—waking or sleeping. This is one of the best ways to accomplish the first of the five steps of dream interpretation. (Step 1: Relate the dream.) After you have written the dream down, read what you have written, then go back and underline the most obvious symbols. (Step 2: Isolate the symbols.) Keep in mind that they will encompass more than persons, places, things or concepts. Symbols can be anything that leaves a strong impression on the dreamer. Among a host of possibilities, they will most certainly include actions and feelings as well.

The following is an example of a sleeping dream with a typically surreal juxtaposition of events. It was chosen for its wealth of symbols. While its complexity makes it impractical to interpret here, you might like to use it as an exercise. If you wish, study it and try to isolate as many symbols as you can before continuing:

In my dream it's really hot and I'm feeling lethargic. For some reason I decide my clothes are soggy. I remove them and walk out onto a kind of porch, except that I'm on the ground level. There's an iron railing—like a fence—and I hang my clothes on it so they'll dry. I look off to my right and see this armadillo walking toward the railing. It comes up and sniffs my clothes, then it lifts its leg like a dog and pees all over my jeans. Actually, I have no idea whether an armadillo could do that. I kind of doubt it, but this one did. That's my dream.

If you challenged yourself to locate the symbols, then you quickly figured out that the "noun" symbols—like railing, clothes and armadillo—were obvious. Probably actions—like removing clothing, hanging them, and peeing—were straightforward, too. Perhaps the descriptive adjectives—words like hot, lethargic and soggy—stood out with equal clarity. But were you aware of a subtler kind of symbol? There were phrases this dreamer used in offhand, almost throwaway asides. They were similar to one another in that each one expressed a sense of being uncertain. These phrases were, "For some reason," "I have no idea" and "I kind of doubt it." The fact that they occurred repeatedly in the dream description makes them especially important symbols, even though they are subtle and aren't a tangible object or an overt activity.

Repeated journaling helps a dreamer tune into the subtleties of dream symbols. It is an exercise useful for familiarizing oneself with the important clues contained in dreams, whether obvious or obscure. The discipline of putting these highly subjective experiences to paper forces the writer to relive the scenes at a mental distance. This allows him to slow down and spend extra time with each symbol. There is no sense of urgency, no feeling of being put on the spot. He can work at leisure, ponder an idea, change his mind and explore various possibilities without pressure.

58

Dream interpretation techniques: Interpreting symbols successfully, while avoiding common pitfalls.

After gaining some facility at recognizing significant symbols, the next step is to choose a symbol or two from each dream and go through the exercise of interpreting it. (Step 3: Interpret the symbols as metaphors.) This is the "Tell me about it!" part. As in the process of recognizing symbols, there are pitfalls with interpretation as well. The most common one is to react emotionally when the "Tell me about it!" question is asked.

Question: Tell me about Brussels sprouts boiled in milk.

Answer: Disgusting!

That is certainly an honest response, but the answer does little to shed light on how the dreamer might define the symbol in the context of his own life. The response desired is roughly halfway between a dictionary definition and an exercise in free association. It's neither completely one nor the other. Regarding an exact definition, dream symbols can be so peculiar that dictionary definitions are difficult to come by. Is there, for example, any dictionary in the world that would have a definition of Brussels sprouts boiled in milk? But it is also true that unchecked free association can lead to a good deal of thought-wandering. It is best when the dreamer gives a response that is succinct and direct.

What is being asked of the dreamer is to explain the symbol in the simplest, most neutral fashion possible. When an emotional answer like "Disgusting!" is given, an excellent remedy is to ask the dreamer to explain the symbol to a small child, especially if the child is a space alien. This technique requires the dreamer to take a step back and offer a more basic and more objective assessment.

Question: I'm only four-years-old, so I have a limited vocabulary. I'm also from Mars, so I have absolutely no knowledge or appreciation of the affairs on Earth. I have no concept of what you've been saying. Could you please tell me about boiling Brussels sprouts in milk and say it in a way that I can understand you?

Answer: Well, Brussels sprouts are small round green things called vegetables. You're supposed to eat them. They're good for you because they're full of vitamins and minerals, which means they can help keep you strong and healthy. The trouble is that they aren't nice to eat. A lot of people stay away from them because they taste bad. That means they're unpleasant. Cooking them in milk is supposed to help. Maybe it does, but I don't think I'd ever want to try it. Just the idea of it makes me feel sick.

As a reader, step back from this explanation for a moment and observe what this dreamer just told himself about nutrition—figurative or literal—and how he intends to deal with that which is "good for you" in his life. Suddenly it is apparent that this dream is a warning: He seems to be telling himself that the idea of doing things that are good for him "makes him sick." The chances are that his dream has nothing whatsoever to do with vegetables, although that might be part of it, too. But it is certainly about an attitude he has toward making constructive and healthy decisions in his life.

Another pitfall is to answer the "Tell me about it!" question with an erudite response.

Question: Tell me about boiling Brussels sprouts in milk.

Answer: Centuries ago, the finest chefs discovered that marinating various gamey-tasting meats in milk leached them of their strong flavors. The same is true of certain vegetables, like Brussels sprouts, which can also be cooked satisfactorily in a salt brine.

That answer certainly represents a knowledgeable response, but it would not be helpful to a pre-school Martian or to the dreamer himself.

To conclude, the two most common pitfalls to interpreting a symbol—reacting emotionally or offering a lofty intellectual response—are best avoided. Ultimately, the most enlightening and helpful symbol definition is one which a small child would understand.

59

Dream interpretation techniques: Working sensitively with someone else.

Whenever one works on a dream, it is extremely important to share and discuss ideas with at least one other thoughtful, but non-intrusive, individual. Input from another person is invaluable. Simply make certain that the rules of non-invasion, discussed in Chapter 28, are respected. In other words, avoid expressing your opinion emphatically if you have an idea about someone else's dream.

When an idea occurs to a listener, he might be animated. Though not intended offensively, the suggestion might be offered in an excited—sometimes overly impassioned—manner. "Oh, I know! You're telling yourself to be gentler with your criticisms." A remark like that may come across as only a suggestion and may be innocuous, but the speaker's tone of voice and attitude might also imply a more authoritative stance. If the speaker is particularly good at figuring out symbols, the dreamer's response might shift from "That's an interesting idea," to, "Oh well, Bob is always right about these things, so we'll just take his word for it." That's when the whole process falls apart. The minute someone is perceived as infallible, he takes the role that Michael assumed in Chapter 52, and the method loses its integrity. That's why introducing one's opinion with "If this dream were mine" is invaluable. It assures that the suggestion never becomes more than simply that: a suggestion.

There is, however, another facet to this. It is not only the person making the suggestion who needs to be vigilant. The dreamer, too, has to be alert. No matter how forcefully or inappropriately a suggestion is made, it is incumbent on the dreamer to receive it as no more than an idea. I recommend that dreamers listen carefully to the suggestion being made, and then pay particular attention to the physical sensations they experience. As odd as it may seem, if the proffered idea has hit the mark, the dreamer might actually feel a physical change in his body. This can come in many forms. One might be aware of one's shoulders. Tension often is held in this area, so if an idea feels right, one's upper body might relax. A deep cleansing breath might also be noted. On occasion, there can be tears.

If, on the other hand, the suggestion is off the mark, it will seem to the dreamer as if he has been listening to nothing more than a mental concept—somebody's hypothesis.

I encourage dreamers to share these kinds of responses with those making the suggestions. When the dreamer lets the commenter know how his interpretation is felt, it has a way of putting extreme and unrestrained remarks back into balance. Consider the following brief exchange:

Forceful suggestion: Oh, I know! You're telling yourself to be gentler with your criticisms.

Dreamer: (after a thoughtful pause) Wow. That really hits home.

This kind of exchange can be powerful and cathartic. Despite the domineering tone of the suggestion, the dreamer sensed that it was accurate, and the parties involved felt good. The dream was understood; the door to change was opened. Yet even in this instance, another quieter message was delivered simultaneously. By taking his time to respond, the dreamer made it clear that the idea presented was not automatically accepted. It was an offering, a proposal, and nothing more. Until it went through the dreamer's own system of internal verifications, it had no more meaning than a series of words. This was a signal to the person making the suggestion that, no matter how emphatic he was being, his forcefulness, in and of itself, was irrelevant.

Now, consider the following where the same exchange produced a different response:

Forceful suggestion: Oh, I know! You're telling yourself to be gentler with your criticisms.

Dreamer: (after a moment's thoughtful pause, and shaking his head) No. That doesn't ring true.

This, too, is a powerful exchange, one in which the suggestion, no matter how autocratically presented, is simply rejected. This acts quickly to curb the strong approach of the suggester. It is embarrassing to vigorously present an idea only to have it summarily dismissed. It is probable that the person making the suggestion will be more careful and less presumptuous the next time: If this dream were mine...

The more people involved, the more likely it will be that someone will recognize an inadvertently aggressive intrusion. Plus, the more people participating, the greater the idea pool when it comes to working constructively with the symbols. Twelve people is about the limit. Groups larger than that become cumbersome and tend to leave participants uninvolved. Nine is better. However, somewhere around six is ideal for a class. A pair of individuals, working independently as a team, is also excellent.

60

Dream interpretation techniques: Putting the dream together.

At some point, after journaling for a while and then tinkering with a few obvious symbol definitions, the dreamer's confidence in the process will grow enough that working on the dream as a whole is the next logical step. It must be emphasized that working on every single symbol is the key to success. It is one reason why dream snippets are useful. Ironically, the fact that part of the dream was lost between sleeping and awakening is far less important than being certain that everything recalled is dealt with. Each symbol adds a unique piece of information; omitting anything can drastically alter the dream's message.

Consider the following example of a short sleeping dream. Note that the first two steps of the dream interpretation process have been accomplished: the dream has been related, and the most important symbols have already been isolated and underlined.

I am out for a stroll. I come to a fork in the road and look at the path going to my left. Suddenly, I get the urge to eat some sushi.

What follows are the dreamer's own definitions of the underlined symbols as he came to Step 3: Interpret the symbols as metaphors.

stroll: going leisurely from one place to another

fork in the road: have to make a decision

path going to my left: My parents came from Italy, and in Italian, the word for "left" also means "sinister." I found that intriguing growing up in the United States, though it never had that strong an association for me. But I guess I do have a sense of the left path being "the forbidden fruit," the mysterious, taboo direction.

suddenly: unexpectedly

urge: strong desire

eat: take in for nourishment

sushi: a food that is foreign to my culture but which I have learned to enjoy

Before reading beyond this paragraph, go back over these symbol definitions and try putting the dream together yourself. (Step 4: Retell the dream, using and owning the metaphors.) See if you can assemble it into a storyline. Start by distilling into its essence the dreamer's lengthy definition of "path going to my left," and don't forget to sprinkle your narrative with a liberal seasoning of "There is a part of me that..."

What follows is the account the dreamer himself came up with.

There is a part of me that is leisurely going from one place inside myself to another. This part of me comes to a fork—a spot where I have to make a choice. I look in the direction of things that I have always considered mysterious and taboo for myself, like forbidden fruit. But unexpectedly, there is a part of me that has a strong desire to take in nourishment that was initially foreign to me but which I have learned to enjoy.

Aren't dreams amazing? All that from the unlikely combination of forks in the road and sushi. During our discussion (Step 5: Explore the dream's relevance in your life.) this dreamer explained his desire to expand beyond the self-imposed, constricting parameters of his life. His dream was giving him permission to do that.

The chances are that the story line you crafted was similar to that of the dreamer's; this dream was reasonably straightforward. Now, as an additional exercise, go back and reconstruct the plot line again. Only this time, leave out one of the symbols. At the very least, doing so will rob the dream of some of its richness, some of its detail. In a worst case scenario it substantially changes the dream's meaning, often leaving an erroneous impression. Fixating on only the most striking aspects of the dream, or worse, on a single symbol—like the symbol of the mistress in Jeremy's dream in Chapter 7—can lead to distortions and accompanying distress. Working on every single symbol in the dream is the key to finding a meaningful interpretation.

61

Dream interpretation techniques: Being sensitive to the unique nature of symbol definitions.

Recall the dream example of forks in the road and sushi in the previous chapter. There is one more idea to explore: How many of us would have come up with this particular definition of "path going to my left?" The word "left" could elicit any number of responses depending on a dreamer's experience and upbringing. In this case, "the left path" is an expression that was, archaically, associated with evil in the Christian belief system. Yet that's not where the dreamer took it at all. The combination of his Italian Catholic parents, coupled with a more eclectic upbringing in the United States, led him to his own unique symbolism.

Supposing during a dream class someone had said to him, "Oh, I know! The left path is evil. You're telling yourself not to go there." What an invasion and an obstruction that would have been! It would have led to exactly the opposite conclusion than the one the dreamer was trying to tell himself.

It is essential to allow a dreamer the comfortable freedom to communicate his own inner thoughts, his own distinct interpretation of his symbols. Certainly, one of the most exhilarating aspects of working with dreams is to witness this phenomenon in action. The results are far more fascinating—and surprising—than imposing an idea on someone. No single person, regardless of how adept at dream interpretation, could possibly come up with as much variety and personal insight as dreamers do on their own.

62

Dream interpretation techniques: Dealing with powerful symbols.

On occasion a dream contains a symbol so compelling that the subsequent discussion is dominated by it. For example, think back to Stan and his encounter with the Doberman Pinschers (Chapter 32). That was an example of a dream symbol so overwhelming to him that it made him physically ill; he ended up in bed in the middle of the day. In instances like Stan's, the symbol is obviously important and should be talked through to the satisfaction of the dreamer.

However, once that goal has been achieved, it is both helpful and advisable to go back and consider each remaining symbol on its own merit. In Stan's case, there were dream metaphors of country roads, fears of dying and several others. Each of them added important clues to the dream message. In general, pay special attention to any symbols that might be neglected. It isn't necessary to weave each one directly into the story line, although that often happens. Simply consider the symbol on its own merit and how it relates, peripherally, to the dream as a whole. You will learn more about the intended message by doing so.

63

Dream interpretation techniques: Working with lengthy dreams.

It can happen that a sleeping dream is so long that it is nearly impossible to work with. For several months, two women, well into their seventies, attended a dream class I taught in California. These two had been close friends since childhood and were inseparable. One of them had the most impressive dream recall of anyone I have ever known, and her dreams seemed to go on forever. It could take her several minutes of non-stop talking to relate one. There would be class members who would develop headaches trying to concentrate on the dream details in order to give her a fair hearing. I would have pages of nearly-illegible notes, and my hand would be cramped. Her friend would become visibly impatient at this interminable monologue, but the dreamer would be oblivious. Eventually, she would quietly say, "And I guess that's about all I remember," at which point her friend would invariably blurt out, "Oh, thank God!"

How can such a dream be dealt with? To conscientiously put attention on every single symbol in a lengthy dream like this takes more concentration and effort than anyone can be expected to give, especially in a single session. Spread out over time it would take days. The irony is that little additional understanding is gained from such an exercise. In exceptionally long dreams, the message tends to repeat itself. Simply picking one particular portion—like an individual scene in a play or movie—and working on all the symbols in that part, is enough to gain a satisfactory understanding of the dream's point. If there is any question about the interpretation that is finally reached, one can take two scenes and work on them independently of each other to see if there is a consistent "message." In the case of this participant, she was simply asked to select an especially compelling section of her dream, and that was what we concentrated on.

64

Dream interpretation techniques: Connecting two seemingly-unrelated story lines.

An important message need not be confined exclusively to the dream itself. It can come from a dream in conjunction with an offhand preamble. A common statement from dreamers who are about to relate a sleeping dream is, "Well this probably doesn't have anything to do with it, but..." and then they proceed to tell about a waking experience that seems to have no connection. However, in almost all such cases, the two stories are directly linked symbolically. The "irrelevant" waking story often provides important missing clues, especially if the sleeping dream can only be remembered as a snippet.

In such cases, an important sign to watch for is a kind of disjointed narration on the dreamer's part. Dreamers are often trying to juggle lots of different ideas and memories at the same time, and their description comes out as a stream of consciousness—often humorous and somewhat oblivious to the difference between what happened to them at night and during the day. The following is a good example, starting with a waking experience that, at first, seemed irrelevant to the dreamer:

I was in the grocery store today and it was really busy. I went to get a shopping cart and there was only one left. I knew right away why no one had picked it. It had one of those wheels that isn't round any more—you know, the kind that goes kuh-whap, kuh-whap, kuh-whap all through the store while you're trying to buy stuff. Really annoying!

Anyway, I don't know why I'm telling you all this because you asked me to tell you my dream, right? And this isn't it. OK. Well, here's my dream; all I remember is a tiny piece of it: I was walking in a grove of holly trees and they were really close together. And the trouble was that I was carrying a balloon and I was so afraid that one of the sharp points on the end of a holly leaf was going to pop the balloon. It was tough because I had to walk so carefully between all these trees crowding around me. That's all I remember. Weird, huh?

In our subsequent discussion, this dreamer was surprised to learn that the two stories, one she had from her waking life while shopping for groceries and the other from her sleeping dream about carrying a balloon, were connected.

After Step 1: Relate the dream, which she did above, she proceeded to Step 2: Isolate the symbols. She isolated the symbols from both her waking and sleeping experience. Then she defined them in Step 3: Interpret the symbols as metaphors, as follows.

First, her waking experience:

grocery shopping: get nourishment

shopping cart: a vehicle that had problems and couldn't go right

Then, the sleeping dream:

balloon: full of nothing but air

holly trees: really beautiful but protective and might burst my bubble

We subsequently linked the two sets of symbols in the fourth step of the dream interpretation process: Step 4: Retell the dream, using and owning the metaphors. What follows is what I said to her.

David: If this dream were mine, I'd ask myself if there was a part of me that was trying to get nourishment, but was having trouble because the vehicle I was using inside myself had

> problems and couldn't go right. In addition, I was carrying around a part of myself that was full of nothing but air. Another part of me that is really beautiful but protective of me was trying to burst this bubble, but I was trying to prevent that from happening.

We then moved on to Step 5: Explore the dream's relevance in your life. I asked her if she was, perhaps, carrying an attitude that was "full of nothing but air." Was it possibly preventing her from being "nourished" in some way? It took a moment of discussion for her to make the connection. But then she talked at length about her tendency in social circumstances to be insincere for the sake of trying to fit in. Often, the people she was trying to impress were ones with whom she had little in common. The real social "nourishment" in her life came from treasured friends whom she had known for a long time. They found her behavior "really annoying" and were "protective" of her (her words). They had begun to confront her about her fake behavior, but she was resisting their efforts. Ultimately, she realized it was a good thing that her "bubble" of fake behavior "might burst."

There was more to this dream, but the main point is that, even though shopping carts during a waking experience seemed to have no bearing on a balloon in a sleeping dream, the two were metaphorically related. That was why the dreamer, subconsciously, narrated the two anecdotes as one story.

65

Dream interpretation techniques: Confronting vivid and shocking symbols.

Don't be horrified by repellant symbolism. Dreams are trying desperately to get a point across. They begin gently, but if there is no response, a few days later they try repeating the message in a stronger fashion. If they continue to be ignored, they eventually make absolutely certain they are noticed, and they do so heedless of the dreamer's sensibilities. Sometimes these disconcerting symbols repeat themselves through several dreams over extended periods of time. Anything that will shock the dreamer into attention is fair game. Particular favorites are issues of violence, a sense of foreboding, inappropriate intimacy and embarrassing bodily functions. The following sleeping dream is a prime example. And be forewarned; the symbols are appalling.

A woman dreamed that she was straddling her boyfriend, lying on top of him, naked and preparing for the physical act of love making. Suddenly, from her vagina, there spewed a projectile of some viscous liquid which splattered directly onto her lover's face, leaving him covered with a yellow, pus-like liquid which she knew, immediately, was infected.

Can you imagine? The poor dreamer was distraught, yet we worked on the symbols in a calm, detached fashion, exactly as if they had been mundane images. She was surprised to learn from her own "Tell me about it!" story that her dream had nothing to do with coitus, but everything to do with intercourse in a more general sense. She revealed that she had been avoiding some confrontational dialogues that were needed to straighten out certain affairs in her life. This evasion on her part had begun to adversely influence other aspects of her daily performance at work and at home. She even began to wonder if her behavior was making her ill.

How easy it would be to skip down the Freudian path with this dream! Was she envious of men with their prominent sexual apparatus? Was she angry at them in general? Did she secretly resent her boyfriend?

Other therapeutic presumptions could be made as well. Did she feel a sense of gender ambivalence? Was she being warned about a physical ailment? Did she represent the Jungian archetype of the harlot?

Those questions, along with others like them, were certainly in the back of my mind as we talked, but I preferred to let her direct the discussion without dictating preconceived ideas. Instead, I simply used her own symbol definitions. Even if the above-mentioned concepts were valid on some buried level, what emerged was more relevant to her in the immediate moment. This woman's growing inability to communicate effectively had made her incapable of taking constructive action in the affairs of her life, and it was leading her to a crisis point. The dream symbols were correct: She had "contaminated" the "intercourse" of her daily life. What's more, if she didn't act on the dream's frantic efforts to grab her attention, she was in danger of worse things happening to her, as her dream—not only the initial sleeping dream, but eventually, when it also began to be expressed as a waking dream—would surely intensify.

All of us are capable of recognizing dream messages early in their communication attempts when the symbols are still gentle. But from time to time, we become too busy, too resistant, too preoccupied, too weary to pay attention. That's when the dream symbols become emphatic and intentionally shock us into paying attention to them.

66

Dream interpretation techniques: Recognizing that the sleeping and waking worlds are blended.

The woman in the last chapter who dreamed that she was straddling her lover, wondered if she was receiving a warning about possible cervical cancer. I replied that sickness was a distinct possibility. Earlier in the book we saw how sleeping dream symbols can appear in the waking lives of dreamers. The rock climber's back-to-back sleeping and waking dreams were good examples (Chapter 44). In the case of this woman and her quasi-sexual dream about social intercourse, it would be foolish of her not to get a thorough pelvic exam.

This brings us back to a subject introduced in Part Seven. We scrutinized the surprisingly thin veil between those occurrences in our outer lives and those "events" that seem to take place within us. While it is difficult to establish any kind of hard and fast rule, there are many cases in which dreams about important issues start subtly and gently as sleeping dreams. If the message is not heard, they try using more emphatic symbols, still while the dreamer is asleep. If that tactic, too, is unsuccessful, they begin shifting to the waking arena. And here's the clincher: They will eventually become as outrageous and appalling in their waking symbolism as they were in their sleeping mode. Like sleeping dreams, the waking ones begin gently, and if the dreamer does not respond, they increase in intensity to the point where they actually can threaten the dreamer's well-being.

Hypothetically, disease of the reproductive organs is an excellent dream symbol for stifled creativity and intercourse. If illness of this kind reaches the point where it threatens an individual's overall health, it is an indication of how long this person has let the situation slide. It is as if the dream were positively screaming in an effort to bring the dreamer to alertness. What's more, if she does not respond, it will observe no boundaries. It may seem shocking, but waking dreams ultimately do not care if the dreamer lives or dies or is maimed or is brought to complete destruction in some other way. The dream's job is to grab the dreamer's attention. It will use whatever is necessary to accomplish that end. In this sense, waking dreams are like a histamine reaction after a toxic insect bite. The histamines are supposed to be helpful, but in some cases, they are excessively powerful and can be more detrimental than the bite was itself. If the dreamer finally hears and pays attention, then the dream has done its job and can rest. If not, it can become absolutely ruthless.

When one has observed numerous examples of the plots and messages of sleeping dreams repeating themselves in waking life, one begins to take such dream-juxtapositions seriously. Dreams mean business, and they can become brutal.

67

Dream interpretation techniques: Finding a dream's relevance in the dreamer's life—unfinished business.

Once a dream, sleeping or waking, has been dissected, and a story line has emerged, how does one use the information? This is Step 5: Explore the dream's relevance in your life. The trick is to remember that dreams are unfinished business.

The concept of unfinished business, first introduced in Chapter 47, is the idea that discomfort or strange phenomena experienced in either waking or sleeping dreams are due to unresolved issues in the dreamer's life. Whether the dream contains commentary on a minor conflict currently at play in the dreamer's world, or a message of profound significance in regard to a life-long pattern, the place to begin hunting for clues is in the thoughts, activities and emotional content of the dreamer's last few days and weeks. What has been on the dreamer's mind? Were there arguments, significant changes at work or at home, new conflicts or crises in his life? Conversely, have things been overly calm; are there subtle feelings of dissatisfaction or incompleteness? Was there a recent reminder of some old, nearly forgotten annoyance or trauma? The chances are the dream is about a present-day, minor issue. But if it turns out to be about something big or long-term, this, too, will become evident simply from an examination of the dreamer's current affairs.

If an issue has been dealt with successfully, then there is no reason for it to be brought to an individual's attention through the dream. Look for unfinished business; that's the key.

68

Dream interpretation techniques: Practicing develops confidence.

So far, we have methodically reviewed the basic tenets of dream interpretation, along with a few inherent pitfalls. The next step is simply to try the method. Don't get discouraged; this takes some practice. Start modestly with a symbol or two. Then work on a short, simple dream. If you have a poignant one that takes pages of notes to record, set it aside for the time being. Or, if you prefer, take one scene that impresses you as being particularly compelling, and work on that. Or better yet, find a willing partner and work on the dream together.

A dream snippet or a short section with only a few symbols is best for starters. Eventually, with repeated efforts, you will build up a sense of the technique. You will quickly recognize the most important symbols, and you will produce clear, helpful interpretations. Practice is the key.

69

Dream interpretation techniques: Acting on the dream's directive.

Using the five steps of the dream interpretation technique reviewed throughout Part Nine gives the dreamer the solution to a riddle that contains a helpful insight. That brings him half way to his goal.

Now comes the harder half: He must act on the dream's message, and that requires change. As a rule we humans do not particularly relish having to work to grow into a better, more wholesome frame of mind. What follows is a good example.

A colleague once inadvertently disturbed a wasp's nest on his way to retrieve his newspaper one summer morning. He was stung so badly that he needed the assistance of paramedics. I visited him during his brief stay in the hospital and he commented, wryly, "I guess you're going to tell me that this is a waking dream." I suggested that, not only was it a dream, but quite an intense one that warranted examination. I suggested that it would be helpful to him to understand the metaphor; there was an important message he was trying to deliver to himself. He replied that he wasn't feeling well enough, yet, but would be sure to contact me as soon as he was home again. Despite his promise, I never heard another word about the incident even though we continued to do business, and there was ample opportunity for a follow-up discussion. It was simply easier for the dreamer to accept his mishap at face value and get on with life as usual.

The irony is that it is precisely this kind of intense, unexpected waking dream that is the easiest to understand and benefit from. When such dreams seem to come charging at us from out of the blue, they usually indicate a relatively fresh problem, one that can be resolved with a simple attitude correction. Certainly the issue has become urgent, but it is not yet entrenched.

Much more difficult to resolve are the dreams that eventually manifest metaphorically as things like long-term physical ailments. When a dreamer comes to me and says that he's had progressive kidney disease for the last decade, or rheumatoid arthritis that no longer allows him to type on his computer, I am less optimistic of a resolution coming from analysis of dream symbols. These diseases are metaphors expressed as disabilities, ones that began trying to communicate with the dreamer years ago. As the hints were ignored, the problems worsened and became chronic.

Yet, even in such cases, I have witnessed a few instances where the dreamer, after repeated attempts to find a cure—or at least to manage the ailment—suddenly heard of a new type of surgery or revisited a formerly overlooked treatment, and the result was significant relief. What made the difference?

It might surprise the reader to understand that unexpected solutions to such medical issues are often accompanied by a noticeable change in the patient's attitude. Sometimes it is simply that the patient becomes discouraged and gives up trying to solve the problem. In the process of this resignation—one that seems like a defeat—there is a form of surrender that takes place. Simultaneously, other entrenched attitudes are dropped; the release of these habitual ways of battling life is all that was ever wanted. The dream has finally been acted on—albeit somewhat haphazardly—and a solution presents itself. But the key is the change that takes place.

Whether one is dealing with angry wasps or chronic diseases or any other invasive waking dream symbol, the resolution comes from conscientiously addressing the dream's message. Waking dreams are not frivolous occurrences; they mean business. If they are important but are ignored, they will return to the dreamer for another attempt at acknowledgement. And next time, they will make an appearance that is more forceful than ever. Eventually they begin to affect his physical wellbeing, often in the form of disease or accidents of one kind or another. The best course is to acknowledge the dream, understand it, and then make the change that is being urged. That combination is what brings a resolution.

PART TEN:

ATTITUDES THAT CAN INTERFERE WITH DREAM INTERPRETATION

Part Ten examines common mental outlooks that undermine dream work.

70

Resistance is a hindrance to successful dream interpretation.

Wouldn't it be nice if change were easy, if we could gain important insights and act on them with no effort? Unfortunately, life seems engineered to make us work hard for every understanding. The dream phenomenon is simple at its core. Its essence can be expressed in the one sentence that has been repeated often throughout this book: Whatever you perceive, is you. But, simple though it may be, the dream is not always easy.

While it can be fun and enlightening, dream interpretation involves a certain amount of hard work. The dreamer has to be thoughtful. More importantly, he needs to be willing to examine his attitudes, knowing that some of them might need to change. Not everyone is willing to subject himself to this kind of examination.

A friend who has followed my dream work for many years was mentoring a bright young woman, a college graduate who was grappling with some personal issues. When the subject of the dream came up in their discussions, the graduate had shown focused interest in the topic, especially the waking dream. The waking dream concept was new to her, and she expressed enthusiasm at the prospect of reading a draft of this book.

I heard nothing for months. Finally, my friend contacted me on a social call. In the course of our conversation I asked about the graduate and how she was faring with the dream. My friend explained that, initially, the interest had been intense. The two had used the dream interpretation method on incidental, relatively unimportant images that had presented themselves in their lives. In this way, they had become familiar with the concept, and had practiced working with the techniques. But when it came time to focus on more intense, personal issues, the graduate balked. As long as the dream was fun and non-threatening—a game that had to do with concerns that she could hold at a distance—she remained enthusiastic. However, one day my friend suggested that it might be time for the graduate to use the dream to take a serious look at the acute conflict she was experiencing with her mother. Perhaps she would learn something about her own participation in the clash, and as a result, find a way to resolve it. That, for all practical purposes, was the end of their experiment with dream interpretation. The moment it became personal, the instant she found that she might have to expose herself to some degree of transparency, it was over.

Any therapist will recognize this type of behavior. In all forms of counseling, resistance is common among patients who aren't ready to face their problems. The same is true for those working with dreams, especially waking dreams. Having to look closely at attitudes and counterproductive behavior patterns can be uncomfortable and distressing. It involves a kind of self-analysis that can become emotionally painful. It takes courage, commitment and discipline to look deeply within oneself. Many are unwilling to endure such close inspection. Thus, resistance can become a significant impediment to helpful dream interpretation.

71

Skimming the surface of dream content is not helpful.

Like any form of therapy, working with the dream necessitates resolute and careful self-scrutiny. If it is to be effective, it cannot be dealt with casually. The tendency is to skim over the surface, coming away with a quick overview. "Just give me the gist of it; that's all I need, and I can fill in the details later." The chances of such an approach being successful are slim. At best, the dream's message will be distorted and inaccurate.

I once received a phone call from a colleague, Ben, who had worked a lot with the dream. He was in the middle of a separation from his wife of thirty years. While negotiating his way through the divorce minefield, he sought assistance from health professionals who, while treating him, also worked with the dream in their own fashion. He called me in consternation after a session with a counselor. A large part of his counselor's approach had to do with "the mirror." In other words, "Look out at the world and you'll see yourself looking back at you." While this vocabulary is somewhat different than what I use, the concept is identical. His counselor was referring to the waking dream, and was using it in an attempt to help. However, Ben was distressed by this therapy session, and called me for assistance. He and his counselor had focused on the soon-to-be ex-wife, and he had been told to remember the mirror. According to the counselor, Ben's wife was a symbol of the conflict he was experiencing, and it was incumbent on him to eliminate her altogether from his life. "She represents the negative."

While there was some truth in the message, the conclusion—a sweeping and unanalyzed generalization—merely skimmed the surface of the dream content, missing the mark by a significant margin. On the phone, Ben and I singled out one symbol—the symbol of his wife—and started working our way through the dream. Because of his familiarity with the process, it went easily.

David: Tell me about your wife.

Ben: She's basically a really good person. Totally faithful. A good mother. We raised a family together and shared a lot of life. I can't exactly say what's happened to us. Maybe we've just changed, gone different ways. I think, somehow, we both know it, too. Things between us have been stale for a long time. But I was the one who brought up getting a divorce, and that started a whole set of reactions. She was really hurt and took it badly. Now there are some games being played. I think she's trying to fight back—hurt me as much as I hurt her. I'm trying really hard not to start a war, but it's difficult, and sometimes I don't react so well either. We get into fights and start yelling at each other.

While any divorce has at least two sides to the conflict, and I was a party to only one of them, I think it is clear, even from this fraction of our conversation, that the blanket remark that Ben's wife "represents the negative" is a misleading oversimplification. I certainly would agree that she is "a mirror" for him—that if he looks carefully at the description he offered, he would learn a lot about himself. However, what he would see reflected back to him would include far more than negative qualities. He would see someone with many good traits, including the quality of nurturing ("a good mother"), steadfastness ("totally faithful"), and someone whose nature includes a sense of fragility and the ability to feel pain ("really hurt and took it badly").

Ben's dilemma was so much more complex and ambivalent than the three-word description that was offered. He clearly saw the goodness in his wife—for many years his primary companion—who had become his adversary. There were also clues to the inevitable struggle that was taking place inside of him. On one level, the whole issue was about some changes that were going on within himself. These changes were being reflected back to him through the symbols of a waking dream.

Ben's experience is an excellent example of what can happen when dreams—either waking or sleeping—are dealt with in an impulsive, unanalyzed or superficial way. Accurately interpreting dreams takes work. The more critical the dreamer's issue, the more uncomfortable the interpretation process can be. It is often this sense of discomfort that causes dreamers to avoid thoroughly analyzing their symbols. But interpreting a dream by skimming its surface is counterproductive. It is better to leave it unanalyzed than to draw erroneous conclusions about a dream's meaning.

72

John and his garden: Not seeing a relationship between a dream and a relevant circumstance in his life, can cause a dreamer to miss the important dream message.

A dilemma occasionally arises when a dreamer can't relate his dream's message to any issue in his life that he is currently grappling with. When an association of this sort is missed, it can seem as if the dream's message is meaningless.

This is a problem not exclusive to dream interpretation. Consider this situation: A father is dismayed when his normally-attentive teenage daughter becomes distracted. She stops doing her chores, her grades plummet, she seems incapable of giving a direct answer to the simplest question. The father tries reasoning, cajoling, disciplining. Nothing works. In increasing alarm, he takes her to the doctor who puts her through a battery of tests—all negative. Finally, during the appointment to discuss the father's medical concerns, the doctor leans back in her chair, takes a deep breath and asks, "Has it ever occurred to you that your daughter might be in love?"

Suddenly, the light dawns. The scattered puzzle pieces fit neatly together, and the father wonders how he could ever have missed all the clues that now seem so obvious.

A connection that should have been clear, was difficult to see—like a clue in a crossword puzzle that is only obvious after you know what the word is. It sometimes takes work on the dreamer's part to find the connection, and not everyone is willing to put in that effort. This is one of the things that can make dream work difficult; the steps are simple, but not always easy.

The next example illustrates this potential problem. I have a neighbor, John, who occasionally presents me with one of his sleeping dreams. During an evening get-together with his wife, he casually related one.

Step 1: Relate the dream.

John: I'm hovering over our vegetable garden. For some reason, I'm holding onto a paper bag—you know, one of those paper grocery bags with the handles. It's full of newspapers headed for the recycling pile. As I look down at the garden, I see a beet that's growing in one spot, off to the side, except that it's growing in such a way that it's about half out of the ground. I don't just see the greens; I can see quite a bit of the root, too. I'm impressed because it's huge. It's about the size of a cantaloupe, and I remember thinking, "That's the biggest beet I've ever seen." I remember having the distinct thought that I needed to take special care of it.

Because John and I have worked on a number of dreams together, our discussions tend to progress without problems. We quickly worked our way through the second part: Step 2: Isolate the symbols. Then, we went straight to the third part of the interpretation process, shown below:

Step 3: Interpret the symbols as metaphors.

David: Tell me about hovering.

John: I wasn't as high as, say, a helicopter, but high enough that I could see the whole garden at once.

David: Tell me about vegetable gardens.

John: Well, they're where you grow stuff—stuff that's good for you. But not only that. Vegetables that you grow yourself taste better. They're fresher when you eat them, so they're probably better for you, too.

David: Tell me about newspapers in a paper grocery bag.

John: Well, newspapers tell you about the world and what's going on in it. And the paper bag, that's how our family stores them when we've read them. These were newspapers that we were done with. We were going to recycle them, so I guess you could say that we were getting ready to give them to a place that would reuse them in a new way.

David: Ok, tell me about huge beets, the size of cantaloupes.

John: Actually, I love beets, but for some reason I've never gotten around to growing them until this year. I'm not sure why. Anyway, they're so nutritious, and I love the taste. And I guess that, since this one was extra big, it had even more taste and even more vitamins than normal.

David: Tell me about having so much of it out of the ground and exposed.

John: You couldn't miss it.

David: Tell me about taking special care of it.

John: It means it's precious, valuable. You have to protect it because it has importance.

As is usual in these sessions, there was a lag while I finished my notes. Then it was on to the next part of the interpretation process:

Step 4: Retell the dream, using and owning the metaphors.

David: John, if this dream were mine, I'd say that there is a part of me that has positioned itself high enough that I can see the entire area where, inside myself, I grow the things that are good for me. These are the things that are tasty, that are the freshest and most nutritious aspects of myself. At the same time I am holding onto the part of me that informs me about my world and the things that are going on in it. Except that what I am holding onto is—and tell me if you agree with my use of these words, John—"old news." I am getting ready to take this old news to a place inside myself that will use it in a new way. While all this is going on, I see something nutritious and delicious in myself that I can't miss. It is something that I have never grown before, but it is growing in a corner of this nurturing place within me. It is something that I really like. It's huge, and I know that it's precious and valuable. I have to protect it, because it has importance.

There was an uncharacteristic silence between us while we pondered this retelling of his dream. After a few minutes had passed, I presented the following for him to consider:

Step 5: Explore the dream's relevance in your life.

David: John, if this dream were mine I'd ask myself what is going on in my life right now. I'd wonder what was growing within me that has the potential to be so important, so nutritious, tasty and significant to me.

John: (after a moment's reflection, and shaking his head) Nothing that I can think of.

David: No recent soul-searching conversations or discussions?

John: Not really.

David: No new thoughts about the nature of life?

John: Can't think of any.

David: (expressing mild surprise) No changes—say—at work?

John: (shaking his head) No.

David: (in mild consternation) Huh! Anything unusual happen to you last weekend?

John: (thinking) Nope. Just spent time working on the house.

David: (pressing gently) No insights this past few days? No shifts in your way of looking at the world in general?

John: (quietly shaking his head)

I found myself quietly frustrated by John's inability to make a connection between his dream and a significant event in his life or to recognize a change in his viewpoint. But his experience is not uncommon. A connection is not always immediately apparent during a dream analysis session. When such connections fail to be drawn, I always wonder if this is the dream that will prove the exception to the rule. I ask myself if this is the set of symbols that will be no more than a series of random images with no message. To reassure myself in such cases, I remind myself that, if the symbols were no more than a haphazard collection of images, it would be a rarity.

In John's case, the obvious connection was provided by his wife who had been listening quietly to our dialogue and who suddenly piped up, “You've started taking yoga. What about that?” There was a moment during which we all sat and let this sink in. I, for one, shook my head in amused disbelief. How can one not remember a change in a life pattern as significant as that one? And yet, as stated, this sort of thing happens from time to time with dream work. John was not being uncooperative. He enjoys working with dreams, but his mind simply did not make a connection between this significant new activity in his life and my questions about recent changes in his outlook. His wife's revelation—obvious to him in retrospect—took him completely by surprise.

Yoga, which was a new activity for John at the time of our conversation, subsequently developed into a serious endeavor. If one were to ask him, today, about the degree of its importance in his life, without hesitation he would put it near the top of his list. He describes it with words like transformational, inspiring, spiritually invigorating.

To this day John refers to his practice metaphorically, as "tending my vegetable garden." When he has a dream of significance, he pays closer attention to the connection between his daily activities and his dream world.

73

When interpreting a dream, how deeply should one probe when seeking its relevance?

In the last chapter, John had a dream about hovering over a vegetable garden. At first, he could see no correlation between that experience and a recent event or attitude shift in his life. With his wife's input, he finally saw a connection between his dream and his new-found passion for yoga. Had his wife and I not pressed the issue, we might have concluded that his dream was simply an entertaining collection of images that presented themselves to him in a curious and vaguely comical fashion.

However, I believe that all dreams contain valid messages. I doubt if there ever is a dream that is simply a haphazard series of random images with no relationship to anything transpiring in the dreamer's life. This is especially so when the analyzed symbols collect themselves into as lucid and profound a picture as John's dream.

Yet, after repeated probing, John was unable to link his dream and his yoga together. That put me in a quandary. In a situation like this, how much questioning is appropriate on my part? If I start verbally digging, at what point can persistence become confrontational or intimidating? When does my own insistent attitude begin to color a dreamer's response?

Persistent inquiry is not a problem unique to dream analysts. If a police detective has evidence and thinks a suspect isn't being forthcoming, how far is it appropriate for him to push before his own pressing questions begin to color the replies?

When the concept of the dream was still relatively new to me, I would probe aggressively if I had the sense that there was more lurking within the mind of the dreamer than was being revealed. Through experimentation I was simply trying to learn as much about the process as I could. But this is unfair. It is actually a form of subtle bullying and has the potential of skewing the results to be in agreement with the analyst's interpretation, rather than the dreamer's. Over time I have learned that, if there is resistance to searching for a dream's message, it's better if I let it be—although I almost always have the feeling that an opportunity is being missed.

In general, I find it important to allow the dreamer as much room as possible—either to pursue a dream's message, or to leave it alone. Pressure can compel a dreamer to want to please and comply, and that can affect his responses. By contrast, when he is allowed the freedom to reflect without someone else's insistence for an immediate reply, he is more likely to discover and share what is truly in his thoughts.

74

It can be discouraging when dreamers request a dream interpretation, but aren't ready to look within themselves.

John (Chapter 71) was initially unable to see the relevance of his dream in relation to his new-found yoga. That roadblock was inadvertent, a temporary mental obstacle. However, there are those who have occasionally set up another type of interpretation hindrance, one that is more deliberate and less productive: they really don't want to look closely at their dreams. For a while I tried working with a dreamer who had excellent recall and tended to dream in spectacular and vivid color. Such dreams would be the envy of many a dreamer. The first time this person related one of her dreams to me, I made my usual concerted effort to be helpful. However, as the question and answer phase progressed, I noticed that her eyes were glazing over as if her thoughts had wandered far away. Finally, after I had studied my notes and presented the, "If this dream were mine..." phase of our discussion, she gave me a more focused look and said, "Actually, what I really like in my dreams are all the bright colors."

Her message was clear: She was indifferent to any analysis we might reach and certainly was uninterested in changing her life through dream work. She enjoyed the dream phenomenon without having to think about it, and though she was delighted to share a description of her colorful dream imagery, she preferred to take the process no further.

Some dreamers, even though they ask for assistance, set up mental obstacles—whether deliberate or inadvertent. They are not ready to become vulnerable and look closely at their lives. On occasion, this has been a source of frustration, especially when I make a conscientious effort to help and am unable to. These days, rather than become discouraged, I am more patient, allowing dreamers the freedom to be as involved or as detached from their dreams as they need to be.

I also remind myself of those whose lives have been altered for the better due to their serious work with dreams. For example, I think back to the profound efforts made by Ellen regarding her divorce (Chapter 13), or Stan and his encounter with the Dobermans (Chapter

32), or Eunice with her unwholesome entanglements with men (Chapter 38). These individuals, and others like them, have been deeply touched and changed for the better; they will never see life in the same way again.

PART ELEVEN:

THE PRACTICAL VALUE OF THE DREAM

Part Eleven describes how the dream is not only a mystical and spiritual concept, but a practical tool.

75

There are important teachers and philosophers in the West who acknowledge the close link between our objective and subjective experiences.

An idea repeated frequently throughout this book is that, as we change, life around us changes as well. This theory implies a model of existence that includes an elusive, mystical quality most of us don't acknowledge. It suggests that objective and subjective experiences are more closely linked than we usually accept, and that there is little difference between what we imagine in our thoughts, what we dream in our dreams and what we experience out in the world.

While many of us in the West consider this a peculiar concept, there are several renowned teachers in spiritual, metaphysical and scientific fields who freely acknowledge its existence. As pointed out earlier in this book, Carl Jung is one luminary who perceives our outer world as less rigid than is usually accepted. The idea of a changeable world is an integral part of his concept of synchronicity and the a-causal connecting principle. In his writings, he comes close to a direct description of waking dream phenomena as I have described them.

Physicist and author, Dean Radin, is another who argues that the distinction we make between what goes on in our psyches and what transpires in the objective world is artificial: "A long-held, commonsense assumption is that the worlds of the subjective and the objective are distinct, with absolutely no overlap. Subjective is 'here, in the head,' and objective is 'there, out in the world.' Paranormal phenomena suggest that the strict subjective-objective dichotomy may instead be part of a continuous spectrum, and that the usual assumptions about space and time are probably too restrictive."[34]

Berkeley-trained anthropologist, Hank Wesselman, on the subject of the illusory nature of the physical world, remarks: "In my work as an anthropologist, I have heard a singular statement regularly repeated in various forms among the indigenous peoples I have lived with across the years—the proclamation that we are all actually dreaming twenty-four hours a day, that the dream world is the real world, and

[34] Radin, Dean; The Conscious Universe; p. 4.

that this physical world we all take so much for granted is a manifestation of the dream, not vice versa."[35]

Physicist, Fred Allen Wolf: "Thus the self/non-self split is responsible for awareness of the universe as 'out there' and awareness of 'in here' or the 'I.' The two are the same experience, for one cannot be aware of 'out there' without simultaneously being aware of 'in here.'"[36]

Author and life-researcher, Michael Talbot: "Virtually all of our commonsense prejudices about the world are based on the premise that subjective and objective reality are very much separate. That is why synchronicities seem so baffling and inexplicable to us. But if there is ultimately no division between the physical world and our inner psychological processes, then we must be prepared to change more than just our commonsense understanding of the universe, for the implications are staggering."[37]

Here is Harvard-trained endocrinologist and spiritual mentor, Deepak Chopra, on the subject of the illusory nature of the objective world: "What you call real is just the mirror of your expectations." And, "Look into the mirror of the world and you will see only yourself."[38]

Hawaiian psychologist, Ihaleakala Hew Len, explains one of the tenets of the Polynesian shamanic healing technique known as Ho'oponopono: "There is no such thing as 'out there.' Everything exists as thoughts in my mind."[39]

Then there is Richard Bach, whose views are among the most extreme of these authors, writing about our interactions with the "solid" world: "You adjust your perceptions to a certain frequency, and call what you see 'this world.' [However,] you can tune yourself to other frequencies whenever you wish."[40] Bach sees our world as one we invent and then change at will. For him, there is no difference between objectivity and subjectivity.

Finally, the grandfather of all twentieth century scientists, Albert Einstein: "A human being is part of a whole, called by us the

---

[35] Wesselman, Hank; The Bowl of Light; p. 83.

[36] Wolf, Fred Alan; The Dreaming Universe; p. 182.

[37] Talbot, Michael; The Holographic Universe; p. 80.

[38] Chopra, Deepak; The Return of Merlin.

[39] Vitale, Joe; Zero Limits; p. 8.

[40] Bach, Richard; Messiah's Handbook.

'Universe,' a part limited in time and space. He experiences himself, his thoughts and feelings, as something separated from the rest—a kind of optical delusion of his consciousness."[41]

Each of these authors made his written observations for a readership in the West, where the tendency is to separate objective and subjective phenomena into "real" and "imagined" experiences. Yet each writer acknowledges the fallacy of that life model. While using different terminology, and while coming from a variety of disciplines, they all see a close link between what we perceive in our imaginations and what we accept as "real" events in our outer world.

---

[41] Einstein, Albert; as quoted in Dean Radin; The Conscious Universe; p. 302.

76

There is a way to harness the link between objective and subjective experiences into a practical tool for living.

Working with dreams—both sleeping and waking—opens up a new realm from which to view life. It leads to an understanding of the paradox—that we live in both an objective and a subjective, metaphoric world simultaneously. In the case of a waking dream, we might face a circumstance that rivets our attention: Stan and his charging Dobermans, for example (Chapter 32). On one hand, he dealt with the practical, objective details of recovering from his shock; he went home, had a stiff drink and took a nap. On the other, he chose to examine the subjective side of the experience by "translating" the waking dream metaphor into language that brought clarification and understanding about his work attitude.

In the last chapter we examined the statements of several teachers in spiritual and scientific fields who argue that there is a link between the subjective and the objective experiences we have in life. Of those quotes, one that seems particularly radical is the statement made by Richard Bach that, "You can tune into another frequency whenever you wish." The fact that Bach, in his writings, has repeatedly made similar remarks without offering his readers a practical method for experiencing this phenomenon, makes it seem as if his concept is extreme. On the contrary, a simple way to "tune into another frequency," is to observe closely the unusual events of our lives understanding them as dreams, as Stan did. He took a traumatic event and used it to catapult himself into a whole new understanding of life's architecture—its paradoxical structure made up of both an objective and a subjective, metaphoric reality.

Without the benefit of retreating into an ashram, or studying with a guru, or choosing to live for years with a spiritually-oriented indigenous culture, we can take a major step toward experiencing the world in a way that is described by the various authors quoted in the last chapter. We can transform perplexing, sometimes incomprehensible events into messages for our growth. And when we learn to rely on these messages, they become a practical, daily support system.

77

The value of the dream is its effectiveness in providing guidance and love.

When one takes a mystical, spiritual concept like the dream and converts it into a practical support system that can be used on a daily basis, it becomes an invaluable tool. The key is to keep the process simple. Yes, dream interpretation requires work plus a desire to make the changes advocated by the dream. However, consider what you gain by making that effort. At the very least there is conflict resolution. Throughout this book there have been many examples of people whose dilemmas have dissipated as a result of their dream work.

In addition, one learns a process of constructive self-analysis. Recall Austin and his cruise control adventure in Chapter 1. His struggles with his dream went a long way toward helping him successfully address a conflict at work. But his adventure took him so much further than that. His entire perspective on life shifted. He became more thoughtful and more at peace with himself. He developed a greater control over his own destiny. For him, the dream was life changing.

The dream is reassuring as well. It provides reliable alerts, warning the dreamer when he is about to take a turn in a hazardous direction. It also encourages him when he is doing something appropriately. For certain, stress levels decrease, and the bewildering play of life events suddenly makes sense.

And there is more—the most profound part of all: When you have an experience in which the world shifts around you, you can never again take life at face value. You continue to deal with it objectively, but now you are "tuned into" its subjective side as well. The days of pretending that the objective world is a rigid, unalterable truth are over.

Surely, at some level, the dream has to be part of the secret of life itself. It begins with complete personal responsibility: I have only myself to answer to for my own actions, my own experiences, my own dilemmas, my own joys, my own conflicts. If I am distressed by what is occurring around me, I have only myself to look to, to bring about a resolution. This way of thinking represents a radical shift in how we generally perceive life, especially for those of us in the West. It takes time to accept and adapt to these ideas, and it involves a complete retraining of our perceptions.

For those who put in the effort, consider the gifts that are gained. One has access to a new tool to use for conflict resolution and self-analysis. There is a greater feeling of calmness with the understanding that life makes better sense than we thought. And one is endowed with a deeper, more profound view of the universe as a well-ordered whole. Combined, these gifts alter the way we approach living: I now engage in life from a greater sense of peace and security. Because of that, it is much easier to be compassionate. I do not perceive of my colleagues, associates and family as adversaries, so love rather than conflict is the basis of my interaction with them. This is truly transformative.

Life is complex. Innumerable accounts tell of individuals who have looked past our Western understanding of objectivity, discovering many pathways to a greater awareness of the mystical, subjective nature of existence. The dream is a compelling road to this understanding. Its beauty lies in its simplicity, its accessibility, its colorful imagery, and its ubiquity. It never stops working, never stops interacting with us, never stops coaching and nudging us in new, constructive directions; we are always dreaming.

APPENDIX A

The five steps of dream interpretation

Step 1 Relate the dream.

Step 2 Isolate the symbols.

Step 3 Interpret the symbols as metaphors.

Step 4 Retell the dream, using and owning the metaphors.

Step 5 Explore the dream's relevance in your life.

APPENDIX B

The three categories of important waking dreams

1 A dream that is shocking

2 A dream that is bizarre

3 A dream with a symbol that repeats more than twice

APPENDIX C

Metaphors in common speech

The following is a random list of sentences in English. They employ images that are often meaningless when taken literally but communicate vividly as metaphors. Imagery is a quintessential part of the communication process and is innate in most languages—perhaps all of them. English lends itself particularly well to metaphor. Other languages make more use of similes. ("She looks like an angel," "It feels like an oven in here.") Most of the following metaphors are familiar to you. The chances are that you use them without even thinking about it. There are many more, but this list serves adequately to show how common the phenomenon is.

I was out surfing the Web. She got ripped off. He was barking up the wrong tree. I've never had a green thumb. Boy, they really took him for a ride! Get the picture? We grilled her on her story. Don't stretch the truth. Try to be first out of the starting gate. His candidacy was a long shot. My birthday's right around the corner. She was thrilled to death. It was a tough nut to crack. We blew them out of the water. Just feel your hands; you're frozen solid. They were in the doghouse. Don't jump the gun. Her job hung by a thread. There are lots of good fish in the sea.

Don't be such a stiff neck! It was a fly-by-night plan. Plant yourself right there and don't move. What an angel! She was clean from stem to stern. It was another thorn in my side. I had to switch hats. She got the hang of it right away. He was the guinea pig for our experiments. I shot myself in the foot. If you step on my toes, I won't bounce back. The car was in cherry condition. That blew me away. It was the God's truth. Check out my new wireless mouse. He came alive after she left. I feel as if my ship is coming in. She was in hot pursuit. Yesterday I was dead to the world. We had to hold down the fort. It rained buckets.

That's just nuts! He was a chicken. We had a ball. That kid is a monster. We got a rise out of them. He bit the dust. She's a ham. The play was panned. He was a fly in the ointment. She was in seventh heaven. It's their rule of thumb. He was over the moon. I had to jump through hoops. I thought she was sincere, but she was on a fishing expedition. Let's tie up the loose ends. There were tons of presents. That movie was a scream. What a shrimp. The politician danced around the issues. He did an about face. They were eating high on the hog. It suddenly dawned on me. She broke his heart. I lost my train of thought. He was a crispy critter. Let's string those ideas together. Love is in the air. Her mood was black.

My computer crashed. This comes with warmest regards. I stepped into my boss's shoes. He had a leg up on it. What a longhair! We went trucking along. She landed the job. Her travels took her to the four corners of the world. He was a fly on the wall during their argument. She had a warm heart. He let the cat out of the bag. What a rotten break. I primed the pump. She conjured that up. He was killing time. She went into her shell. He came roaring into the room. He was on solid ground. It was a living nightmare. It was her deep-seeded belief. That was a tall order. He lost his head. She was stuck in a rut. They got Shanghaied. He got frost bite. The handwriting was on the wall. It was music to my ears. She was lost in a fog.

What a cold cucumber! She just fell apart. He lost his marbles. It's a figure of speech. He was thick-headed. We turned up the heat on them. He kept those appointments religiously. What a weasel! They were involved in whirlwind negotiations. Keep a lid on it. That beggars the imagination. Turnabout is fair play. That's a pipe dream. She made a good point. As it turned out, I was wrong. Try that on for size. That's nothing but pie in the sky. It was a new piece of the puzzle. He was waiting in the wings. The system had bugs in it. The issue was left up in the air. He went back to the drawing board. The stage play was a riot. She was having her cake and eating it too.

He tried to railroad his point of view. She presented a false front. In my book, that's OK. That news item is sexy. It was a hot tip. He was a square peg in a round hole. Hold your horses. Don't fly off the handle. He has the world at his feet. The paintings were hung cheek by jowl. They rubbed salt in her wounds. He had a prominent cowlick. That's hogwash! He got hung out to dry. She was juiced up. The lawyers presented an open and shut case. She was a magnet. He wasn't playing with a full deck. She fell in love. Good grief! He wasn't the sharpest knife in the drawer. Let's put that idea on ice. It was water off a duck's back. He was green with envy. That stuck in my craw.

Life was weighing her down. He was rattled. That was a hard pill to swallow. She was on the long road to success. We have to nip that in the bud. He wasn't wrapped too tight. He lost his marbles. She was lead-footed. That was over his head. Just let go of all your worries. The truth finally started to sink in. She was out to lunch. It was a wallet-wilting invoice. He wiped the slate clean. They established deep roots. She opened a Pandora's box of ill will. We got the issue ironed out. I got burned on the deal. It was time to come up for air. They went over it with a fine toothed comb. He got into the act.The room got really toasty. He fell in line. Get off the phone! We need to prime the pump. She was hooked.

He blew his top. They had to dust off their playing skills. I'll go draw a bath. There was a cap on spending. His goose was cooked. She was on board with the program. He went to the top of his class. She counted her chickens before they hatched. They'll have to pay the piper. She dragged him into the conference room. He got himself into a jam. It was a tall order. Her eyes were bigger than her stomach. Let's cut a rug! Don't make a mountain out of a molehill. We need to look for greener pastures. She was called on the carpet. Make hay while the sun shines.

I was left stewing in my own juices. This model is top of the line. He dropped the ball on the negotiations. Don't rain on my parade. She was a bad apple. He was a fish out of water. They got raked over the coals. My leg fell asleep. He threw the match. It was the long arm of the law. My boyfriend dumped me. Don't burn any more bridges. That blew my mind. The suspense was killing everybody. The opportunity was staring her in the face. He was the cat's pajamas. On further review, this sentence has a dangling participle. Get a handle on it! Her hands were tied. You really got under my skin. She was at the top of her game.

Sink your teeth into that. They gave her the run around. Our paths crossed. I try not to get into those discussions. He was on his last legs. I kept him at arm's length. She's been around the block once or twice. I'm wiped out. On the other hand, it was fair. His silence spoke volumes; it was deafening. Quit fiddling around! It was curtains for the project. The decision was music to her ears. The football team got the crap kicked out of them. We heard it through the grapevine. I ought to tan your hide. She told a vintage joke. It's time to wake up and smell the roses. We had to dance to a different tune.

It's the best thing to come down the pike in years. He was top dog. She was leader of the pack. It was a stressful day and we all needed a night cap. What an odd duck! They got wind of it. That rings true. He had to run an errand. I was totally wigged out. She had to bang her head against a wall. Better listening was the key to understanding. Did you have to rub his nose in it? He was rusty. They saw the fruit of their labors. She was nettled. He was cruisin' for a bruisin'. We plowed through dinner in a hurry. They took me for a ride. His achievement was a milestone. They were full of shit. We had to go for broke on the deal. Don't rest on your laurels. Just sit on your decision for a while. That threw me for a loop. Her nose was out of joint.

You have to track down the information. We lived in her shadow. He got reamed. They seemed to be backsliding. It'll knock your socks off. She successfully homed in on the problem. They were playing hardball. White man speak with forked tongue. We had to tap into their accounts. What a chatterbox! We put the plan back on the drawing board. You have to let the axe fall where it may. She ran hot and cold. He blew his stack. The book was a potboiler. He was on the threshold of a great achievement. It was the turd in the punchbowl. She was aping his movements. He was really moonfaced. The Lakers squashed the Bruins. She was on top of the world. I'm afraid he took a bath on the business deal. The case was hung up on a technicality. That's a real can of worms. It dealt a blow to her prestige. They threw us a curveball. She performed an impressive juggling act with her schedule. The relationship was thrown into turmoil. He paid a steep price for his arrogance.

She handled the dispute gently. The business had a one-size-fits-all mentality. Hi, Honey! It was a one-night stand. If the shoe fits, wear it. It was time to spread the word. Her anger was simmering. We were all tired and started to fade. Don't mince words. I got stood up. They were on fire with enthusiasm. She was the salt of the earth. That guy was really wired. I was plum tired out. He froze his butt off. Keep your nose to the grindstone. I was totally blown away. We were on pins and needles. Give them the whole nine yards. We were out exploring the web. She was on cloud nine. The story didn't add up. He was cutting up at the party. What a windbag! We have to tackle the problem. I'll knock your block off. She went overboard with her criticism. The negotiations were a soap opera. You have to buckle down. We wormed it out of him. In the long run, it was for the best.

She was an excellent backboard to bounce our ideas off of. I'm stuffed!

Let's rip that CD to the PC music library. I'll give you a buzz when I'm free later today. The whole problem blew up in his face. My car wasn't running. She stole the show. What's cooking? I'm swamped until Thursday. Be sure to cover your bases. What a skunk! He was feeling his oats. What's on your plate for tomorrow? It scared me to death. She turned a corner in her health. It was a visual feast. You were a sight for sore eyes. The blush is off the rose. He was armed to the teeth. He stepped down as CEO.

She didn't have a leg to stand on. It was a tough row to hoe. The event was an eye opener. He was tending to business. The boy was really stuck up. Her elevator doesn't go all the way to the top floor. He became unhinged. The news leaked out. She was at the peak of her career. We won by the skin of our teeth. I didn't buy her answer. Let's scope out the situation. They needed to take steps to fix the problem. There was trouble in the teepee. Let's conjure up a new plan. I have to go home and do some wood shedding. Knock 'em dead, champ! Don't be nosey. It should pan out. He was tight fisted. The family banded together. The issue was a hot potato.

He cleaned up in Vegas. It was a red herring. She is a diamond in the rough. I couldn't stomach it. He elbowed his way in. All hands on deck! I had to pinch hit for my sick colleague. His hands were full. We got hoodwinked. That was the buzzword. What’s up? He was cruising for chicks. They finished him off. Lighten up! The answers were far afield. They looked high and low for it. The laughter died out. She had a twinkle in her eye. He had a different spin on things. It was a mountain of paperwork. Their spirits were broken.

Quit lording it over us! She jumped to the task. The room was bugged. He was burdened with a heavy yoke. She was snowed under. He came up with a great line. He took a stab at the problem. She illustrated her point. His plan went up in smoke. He told a bald-faced lie. The children were chilled to the bone. It was a fucking disaster. She was shaking in her boots. Keep that thought in the back of your mind. I had to let the news sink in. They were stuck in a rut. The singer belted it out. He was the mob's kingpin. She was the bee’s knees. The advice hit home. Did that ring any bells? He seasoned his critique with sarcasm.

She came to a fork in her career. That tough guy meant business. It was not for the fainthearted. We were up at the crack of dawn. He was beside himself with fear. Everyone laughed at the punch line. The prosecution painted a different picture. The comparison was a stretch. The humanitarian program was on the chopping block. It will be the death of me. She had to step aside from management of the company. The plan was a leap into the abyss. He had blood on his hands. She blew the opportunity. They took stock of the situation. Her hands were full. They came down with a bug. We were in the groove. She got my goat. He peeled off his clothes. It was a Mickey Mouse solution.

They beat the tar out of him. It was no cake walk. I could eat you up. Stick around! I'll have a virgin daiquiri, please. Let's wrap this up. The town was an oasis in the middle of nowhere. The game was rigged. That car was a lemon. She was a viper. Don't switch horses in mid-stream. We'll succeed come hell or high water. He worked his butt off. She was no shrinking violet. Let's just plow through the material. He didn't know his ass from a hole in the ground. She was a knockout. They threw in the towel. It was a pregnant pause. She was on a roll. The suggestions were all over the map.

We were on our own stomping grounds. Kick up your heels and party hearty! He tended to score with chicks. My scheme backfired. I spaced out on the question. His new power was intoxicating. She picked up some French on her trip to Paris. Hold your fire! He wriggled out of his commitment. She went off the deep end. His remark hit home. She took the ball and ran with it. Fish or cut bait. We saw a murder of crows. I couldn't fathom his objection. It's the Holy Grail of business. Trouble was brewing. Our discussion flowed smoothly. Don't be an egghead! She had a bee in her bonnet. What a bunch of turkeys! Sunday's sermon was endless. It was a Hail Mary plan, with no chance of success. Give me a thumbnail description. We let the news sink in. He keeps putting up roadblocks. I'm tuned into you. The tenor belted out the high notes. My brother was the runt of our litter. Try to exercise some self-control. It's the nature of the beast. She was a Wednesday's child.

Wealth and rich food resulted in some padding on his tummy. Quit ragging on my buddy! Let's spice up our lives. Stick around. Try to stay on top of it. He was hardnosed. Do it if it floats your boat. Class today was a real grind. We were walking on eggshells. We have to shepherd our plan through the subcommittee. In the first place, it's wrong; in the second place, it's dumb. Put a cap on your spending. She made a big splash. That drink will knock the stuffing out of you.

We'll just have to go with the flow. It was over his head. I held my breath through the proceedings. He took payment under the table. She had ideas dancing in her head. My life is righting itself. Her blood froze. That problem is plaguing me. The situation is well in hand. They could do it in a pinch. It came out of the blue. I don't know if we can pull it off. He was in a pickle. We left her to stew in her own juices. That was the meat of the matter. He got shafted. She enjoyed the fruit of her labors. His eyes glazed over. Up next, we have a great act. They went digging for clues. They wrote me off. We live in the land of milk and honey. He let the news sink in. There was light at the end of the tunnel.

The problem reared its ugly head. We went at a breakneck pace. It was an excellent framework for us. It happens once in a blue moon. Let's take a break. That idea came out of left field. The words simply leaped onto the page. They doctored the numbers. The cop pulled out his revolver and shouted, "Freeze!" I was revved up for the game. She bloomed in her youth. He exploded onto the scene. All the signs pointed to success. Don't play games with me. He took it on the chin. She saw life through a different lens. Shit or get off the pot. They beat him within an inch of his life. We all drifted over to the Coke machine. We'll have to eat the cost. Quit bugging her! Life's a breeze. The movie had a cult following. I smell a rat! She was spoiled rotten. We have to get into high gear.

You have success written all over your face. He marches to the beat of a different drummer. She's so beautiful, men fall all over her. I had to put my editor's hat on. We had a blast. The calculations were dead on. Read the fine print. That won't fly. Those years were a sweet slice of life. He opened up a Pandora's Box of complications. She was walking on air. I saw cracks in her veneer. Don't worry; the sky won't fall. As it stands now, we'll continue as planned. We took the redeye from Seattle to Boston. He let the business slide. What a pain in the butt! She was the big cheese. Keep your head above water.

May I bounce an idea off you? The project rolled right along. I lost my shirt on the deal. Quit your belly-aching! It was a bone of contention. I recommend that you deep six the whole idea. Let the chips fall where they may. His reaction was over the top. I have to brush up on my

French. It was a close shave. They felt hemmed in. She hammered home her point. It was the last leg of her journey. We turned on a dime. She was the cat's meow, and turned me on! He was my knight in shining armor. I'll get out of your hair. My successor was waiting in the wings. That was totally cool!

Don't put all your eggs in one basket. You need to spell out your ideas. Her arguments echoed the truth. I got his stamp of approval. He quit smoking cold turkey. She was in the hot seat. That boggles the mind. We can lick this problem. Is your head screwed on straight? He danced his way into that dubious explanation. My cell phone died. Her ideas were far out. It's time to face the music. Don't poke fun at them. It was a snapshot of his life. The athletes were chomping at the bit. She came up with a solution. I tell you this from the bottom of my heart. The topic was over their heads. He shot me down. We were glued to the TV. He has a tendency to trip over his words. That ended on an exciting note. It'll grow on you. He was torn. That's a scream. The proposal was canned. We chewed the fat. The subject came up. Welcome to our neck of the woods. I'll drop you a line. Just hold on.

We need to harness the energy. Knock it off! We were surprised when she piped up. Suddenly, the light dawned. I need to take a leak. They were convulsed in laughter. I'm going to brain you! Her idea rocks. There's dirty work afoot. What a tight-ass. They cooled their heels in jail. The shit hit the fan. He muddied the issue. That's a two-way street. Let's hit the road. It blew my mind. We ditched the plan. Don't be a wet blanket. It was clear that he was the one calling the shots. They latched on to our idea. Watch your Ps and Qs. It was a chain around my neck. We jumped in with both feet. They had a lot of steam built up around the issue. She never skipped a beat. Don't step over the line. We were throwing around suggestions. I saw my shrink. He chewed me out. He was busting his butt. It was training under fire. Yesterday, she poured the type for her new book. The news shook me up. They skipped town. The decision is coming up. We don't have a dog in that fight. He played second fiddle.

I had a field day compiling this list; it's a lot to chew on. I rest my case.

BIBLIOGRAPHY

Books and Articles

Adams, Kate & Hyde, Brendan; "Grief Dreams And The Theory Of Spiritual Intelligence." Washington DC: Educational Publishing foundation. Dreaming—The Journal Of The Association For The Study Of Dreams, Volume 18, Number 1, 2008.

Avery, Mike; The Secret Language Of Waking Dreams. Minneapolis, MN: Eckankar, 1992.

Bach, Richard; A Gift Of Wings. New York, NY: Dell Publishing Co. Inc, 1975.

Bach, Richard; Messiah's Handbook—Reminders For The Advanced Soul. Charlottesville, VA: Hampton Roads Publishing Company, Inc, 2004.

Bowman, Carol; Children's Past Lives—How Past Life Memories Affect Your Child. New York, NY: Bantam Books, 1997.

Braden, Gregg; Fractal Time. Carlsbad, CA: Hay House, Inc, 2009.

Campbell, Joseph; An Open Life—Joseph Campbell In Conversation With Michael Toms. Burdett, NY: Paul Brunton Philosophic Foundation, 1988.

Campbell, Joseph; Pathways To Bliss. Novato, CA: New World Library, 2004.

Campbell, Joseph; The Power Of Myth—With Bill Moyers. New York, NY: Random House, Inc, 1991.

Cannon, Delores; Jesus and the Essenes. Huntsville, AR: Ozark Mountain Press, 1992.

Chopra, Deepak; The Return Of Merlin. United Kingdom: Random House UK Ltd, 1995.

Collins, Kathryn Terah; The Western Guide To Feng Shui—Room By Room. Carlsbad, CA: Hay House, 1999.

Dass, Ram; Still Here—Embracing Aging, Changing, And Dying. New York: Penguin Putnam, Inc, 2000.

Doyle, James M; True Witness. New York, NY: PALGRAVE MACMILLAN, 2005.

Dyer, Wayne; Real Magic—Creating Miracles In Everyday Life. New York, NY: HarperCollins Publishers, 1992.

Eisler, Riane; The Chalise And The Blade—Our History, Our Future. San Francisco, CA: Harper & Row, Publishers, 1987.

Emoto, Masaru; The Hidden Messages in Water. Translated by David A. Thayne. Hillsboro, OR: Beyond Words Publishing, Inc, 2004.

Emoto, Masaru; Love Thyself—The Message From Water III. Translated by Masayo Hachii. Carlsbad, CA: Hay House, Inc, 2004.

Evans-Wentz, W. Y; Tibet's Great Yogi Milarepa—A Biography From The Tibetan. London: Oxford University Press, 1969.

Feild, Reshad; Breathing Alive. Rockport, MA: Element, Inc, 1991.

Fontana, David; The Secret Language Of Dreams—A Visual Key To Dreams And Their Meanings. London: Duncan Baird Publishers, 1994.

Garfield, Patricia; Creative Dreaming. New York: Ballentine Books, 1974.

Goldsworthy, Adrian; Caesar—Life Of A Colossus. New Haven, CT: Yale University Press, 2006.

Grasse, Ray; The Waking Dream—Unlocking The Symbolic Language Of Our Lives. Wheaton, IL: Quest Books, 1996.

Ingram, Julia & Hardin, G. W; The Messengers. New York, NY: Simon & Schuster, Inc, 1996.

Johnson, Linda; The Complete Idiot's Guide To Hinduism. New York, NY: Alpha Books. 2002.

Jung, C. G; Dreams. Translated by R. F. C. Hull. Princeton, NJ: Princeton University Press, 1974.

Jung, C. G; Memories, Dreams, Reflections. Recorded and edited by Aniela Jaffé. Translated from the German by Richard and Clara Winston. New York, NY: Random House, 1963.

Jung, C. G; On The Nature Of The Psyche. Translated by R. F. C. Hull. Princeton, NJ: Princeton University Press, 1973.

Jung, C. G; Syncronicity—An Acausal Connecting Principle. Translated by R. F. C. Hull. Princeton, NJ: Princeton University Press, 1969.

Jung, C. G; Word And Image. Edited by Aniela Jaffé. Princeton, NJ: Princeton University Press, 1979.

Keeney, Bradford; The Bushman Way Of Tracking God. New York, NY: Simon & Schuster, 2010.

Kovacevic, Filip: "A Lacanian Approach to Dream Interpretation." Washington, DC: Dreaming—Journal of the Association for the Study of Dreams, Volume 23, Number 1, March 2013.

LaBay, Mary Lee; Past Life Regression—A Guide For Practitioners. Victoria, BC: Trafford, 2004.

LaBerge, Stephen & Rheingold, Howard; Exploring The World Of Lucid Dreaming. New York, NY: Ballantine Books, 1990.

LaBerge, Stephen; Lucid Dreaming—A Concise Guide To Awakening In Your Dreams And In Your Life. Boulder, CO: Sounds True, Inc, 2004.

Laszlo, Ervin; Science And The Akashic Field. Rochester, VT: Inner Transitions, 2007.

Living Bible—Catholic Edition. Wheaton, IL: Tyndale House Publishers, 1984.

Merrifield, Jeff; Damanhur—The Story Of The Extraordinary Italian Artistic And Spiritual Community. Santa Cruz, CA: Hanford Mead Publishers, Inc, 1998.

Montangero, Jacques; "Using Dreams in Cognitive Behavioral Psychotherapy: Theory, Method, and Examples." Washington, D.C: Educational Publishing Foundation. Dreaming—Journal of the Association for the Study of Dreams, Volume 19, Number 4, 2009.

Moss, Robert; Conscious Dreaming. New York, NY: Three Rivers Press, 1996.

Myss, Caroline; Sacred Contracts. New York, NY: Three Rivers Press, 2002.

Newman, Zoe; "Bringing A Dreamwork Lens To Everyday Life: Relationships As Waking Dreams." Berkeley, CA: Dream Time—A Publication Of The International Association For The Study Of Dreams, Volume 27, Number 1, Winter 2010.

Newman, Zoe; Lucid Waking. Berkeley, CA: White Egret Press, 2010.

Newton, Michael; Memories Of The Afterlife. Woodbury, MN: Llewellyn Publications, 2013.

Norbu, Chögyal Namkhai; Dream Yoga And The Practice Of Natural Light. Edited by Michael Katz. Ithaca, NY: Snow Lion Publications, 1992.

Osbon, Diane, K; A Joseph Campbell Companion—Reflections On The Art Of Living. New York, NY: HarperCollins Publishers, 1991.

Perls, Frederick S; Gestalt Therapy Verbatim. Compiled and edited by John O. Stevens. Lafayette, CA: Real People Press, 1969.

Radin, Dean; The Conscious Universe—The Scientific Truth Of Psychic Phenomena. New York, NY: HarperCollins Publishers, 1997.

Richter, Conrad; The Fields. New York, NY: Bantam Books, 1965.

Rinpoche, Tenzin Wangyal; The Tibetan Yogas Of Dream And Sleep. Edited by Mark Dahlby. Ithaca, NY: Snow Lion Publications, 1998.

Roach, Mary; Spook. New York, NY: W. W. Norton & Company, 2005.

Rubinstein, Arthur; My Many Years. New York, NY: Alfred A. Knopf, 1980.

Shainberg, Catherine; Kabbalah And The Power Of Dreaming—Awakening The Visionary Life. Rochester, VT: Inner Traditions, 2005.

Singh, Jaideva; Pratyabhijnahrdayam—The Secret Of Self-Recognition. Delhi, India: Motilal Bandarsidass Publishers Private Limited, 1963.

Singh, Thakar; The Way of Life 2002. Umpqua, OR: Edition Naam USA, 2002.

Sturzenacker, Gloria; "The Ullman Method Of Group Dreamwork." Berkeley, CA: Dream Time—A Publication Of The International Association For The Study Of Dreams, Volume 29, Number 2, Spring 2012.

Shakespeare, William; The Annotated Shakespeare, Volume III, The Tragedies and Romances. Edited by A. L. Rowse. United Kingdom: Orbis Publishing Ltd, 1984.

Sheldrake, Rupert; A New Science Of Life—The Hypothesis Of Morphic Resonance. Rochester, VT: Park Street Press, 1981.

Stevenson, Ian; Unlearned Language—New Studies In Xenoglossy. Charlottesville, VA: University Press of Virginia, 1984.

Storch, Tanya; "Ten Years Of Teaching Dream Analysis At The University Of The Pacific." Berkeley, CA: Dream Time—A Publication Of The International Association For The Study Of Dreams, Spring 2011.

Talbot, Michael; The Holographic Universe. New York, NY: HarperCollins Publishers, 1991.

Tigunait, Pandit Rajmani; At The Eleventh Hour-The Biography of Swami Rama. Honesdale, PA: Himalayan Institute Press, 2001.

Tolle, Eckhart; The Power of Now. Novato, CA: New World Library, 1999.

Trowbridge, Bob; The Hidden Meaning of Illness—Disease as a Symbol & Metaphor. Virginia Beach, VA: ARE Press, 1996.

Tucker, Jim B; Life Before Life—A Scientific Investigation Of Children's Previous Lives. New York, NY: St. Martin's Press, 2005.

Villoldo, Alberto; Courageous Dreaming—How Shamans Dream The World Into Being. Carlsbad, CA: Hay House, Inc, 2008.

Vitale, Joe; Zero Limits--The Secret Hawaiian System For Wealth, Health, Peace, And More. Hoboken, NJ: John Wiley & Sons, Inc, 2007.

Walsch, Neale Donald; Conversations With God—an uncommon dialogue, Book 2.

Charlottesville, VA: Hampton Roads Publishing Co, 1997.

Watkins, Mary; Waking Dreams. Dallas, TX: Spring Publications, Inc, 1988.

Watson, Lyall; Gifts Of Unknown Things—A True Story Of Nature, Healing, And Initiation From Indonesia's "Dancing Island." Rochester, VT: Destiny Books, 1991.

Webster, Richard; Practical Guide To Past-Life Memories. St. Paul, MN: Llewellyn Publications, 2001.

Wesselman, Hank; The Bowl Of Light. Boulder, CO: Sounds True, Inc, 2011.

Wolf, Fred Alan; The Dreaming Universe. New York, NY: Simon and Schuster, 1994.

Yogananda, Paramahansa; Autobiography Of A Yogi. Los Angeles, CA: Self-Realization Fellowship, 1998.

Recorded Media References

Arntz, William & Chasse, Betsy; What the Bleep Do We Know!? Beverly Hills, CA: Twentieth Century Fox, 2004.

Chopra, Deepak; Ageless Body, Timeless Mind. New York, NY: Random House Audio, 1993.

Chopra, Deepak: Journey To The Boundless. Niles, IL: Nightingale Conant; audio cassettes, 1996.

Das, Lama Surya; Tibetan Dream Yoga—A Complete System for Becoming Conscious in your Dreams. Boulder, CO: Sounds True, 2000.

Dyer, Wayne W. & Chopra, Deepak; Creating Your World The Way You Really Want It To Be. Carlsbad, CA: Hay House; audio cassettes, 1998.

Howard, Don; Albert Einstein: Physicist, Philosopher, Humanitarian. Chantilly, VA: The Teaching Company; Course # 8122, 2008.

Keating, Thomas; The Contemplative Journey—Volume One. Boulder, CO: Sounds True, 1997.

Keating, Thomas; The Contemplative Journey—Volume Two. Boulder, CO: Sounds True, 1997.

Tolle, Eckhart; Awakening in the Now. Eckhart Teachings, Inc; www.eckharttolle.com

Internet References

http://en.wikipedia.org/wiki/Artemidorus

http://en.wikipedia.org/wiki/Synchronicity

http://en.wikipedia.org/wiki/Totem

http://www.En.wikisource.org/wiki/One_Hundred_Poems_by_Kabir.html

http://psychology.about.com/od/sensationandperception/a/color_pink.html

http://webspace.ship.edu/cgboer/boss.html

http://www.angelfire.com/journal/worldtour99/sapirwhorl.html

http://www.brainyquote.com/quotes/authors/a/albert_einstein.html

http://www.brainyquote.com/quotes/authors/j/joseph_campbell.html

http://www.brainyquote.com/quotes/quotes/j/josephcamp141568.html

http://www.ehow.com/info_8428616_effects-colors-moods.html

http://www.fox8.com/wjw-reincarnation-txt,0,1190900.story

http://www.goodreads.com/quotes/show/267871

http://www.jewishvirtuallibrary.org/jsource/judaica/ejud_0002_0015_0_15400.html

http://www.lucidity.com/NL53.ResearchPastFuture.html

http://www.michaellennox.com

http://www.oaks.nvg.org/eg4ra13.html

http://www.paranormalresearchsociety.org/overview-history

http://www.reincarnationforum.com

http://www.Sufism.org/lineage/rumi/rumi-daylight-tr-by-kabir-camille-helminski-excerpts-2.html

http://www.world-of-dreaming.com/novadreamer.html

http://www.world-of-lucid-dreaming.com/lucid-dreaming-blog.html

http://www.youtube.com/watch?v=_EWwzFwUOxA

http://www.youtube.com/watch?v=5965wcH2Kx0&feature

ABOUT THE AUTHOR

Author, David Rivinus, began studying dream analysis in the early 1970s while working at an outpatient mental health clinic in eastern Indiana. Since then he has facilitated classes and workshops throughout the United States, Western Europe and the Americas. A long-time member of the International Association for the Study of Dreams, he was a presenter at their annual conference in Berkeley, CA in 2012. He belongs to several dream-related online chat groups, including blogs on lucid dreaming. He currently lives in Portland, OR.

For more information, please visit www.teacherofdreams.com or email the author at david@teacherofdreams.com.

Other Books By Ozark Mountain Publishing, Inc.

Dolores Cannon
Conversations with Nostradamus,
Volume I, II, III
Jesus and the Essenes
They Walked with Jesus
Between Death and Life
A Soul Remembers Hiroshima
Keepers of the Garden.
The Legend of Starcrash
The Custodians
The Convoluted Universe - Book One,
Two, Three, Four
Five Lives Remembered
The Three Waves of Volunteers and the
New Earth
The Search for Hidden, Sacred
Knowledge
Stuart Wilson & Joanna Prentis
The Essenes - Children of the Light
Power of the Magdalene
Beyond Limitations
Atlantis and the New Consciousness
The Magdalene Version
O.T. Bonnett, M.D./Greg Satre
Reincarnation: The View from Eternity
What I Learned After Medical School
Why Healing Happens
M. Don Schorn
Elder Gods of Antiquity
Legacy of the Elder Gods
Gardens of the Elder Gods
Reincarnation...Stepping Stones of Life
Aron Abrahamsen
Holiday in Heaven
Out of the Archives – Earth Changes
Sherri Cortland
Windows of Opportunity
Raising Our Vibrations for the New Age
The Spiritual Toolbox
Michael Dennis
Morning Coffee with God
God's Many Mansions
Nikki Pattillo
Children of the Stars
A Spiritual Evolution
Rev. Grant H. Pealer
Worlds Beyond Death
A Funny Thing Happened on the Way to
Heaven
Maiya & Geoff Gray-Cobb
Angels - The Guardians of Your Destiny
Maiya Gray-Cobb
Seeds of the Soul
Sture Lönnerstrand
I Have Lived Before
Arun & Sunanda Gandhi
The Forgotten Woman
Claire Doyle Beland
Luck Doesn't Happen by Chance
James H. Kent
Past Life Memories As A Confederate
Soldier
Dorothy Leon
Is Jehovah An E.T
Justine Alessi & M. E. McMillan
Rebirth of the Oracle
Donald L. Hicks
The Divinity Factor
Christine Ramos, RN
A Journey Into Being
Mary Letorney
Discover The Universe Within You
Debra Rayburn
Let's Get Natural With Herbs
Jodi Felice
The Enchanted Garden
Susan Mack & Natalia Krawetz
My Teachers Wear Fur Coats
Ronald Chapman
Seeing True
Rev. Keith Bender
The Despiritualized Church
Vara Humphreys
The Science of Knowledge
Karen Peebles
The Other Side of Suicide
Antoinette Lee Howard
Journey Through Fear
Julia Hanson
Awakening To Your Creation
Irene Lucas
Thirty Miracles in Thirty Days
Mandeep Khera
Why?
Robert Winterhalter
The Healing Christ
James Wawro
Ask Your Inner Voice
Tom Arbino
You Were Destined to be Together
Maureen McGill & Nola Davis
Live From the Other Side
Anita Holmes
TWIDDERS
Walter Pullen
Evolution of the Spirit
Cinnamon Crow
Teen Oracle
Chakra Zodiac Healing Oracle

For more information about any of the above titles, soon to be released titles,
or other items in our catalog, write or visit our website:
PO Box 754, Huntsville, AR 72740
www.ozarkmt.com

Other Books By Ozark Mountain Publishing, Inc.

Jack Churchward
Lifting the Veil on the Lost Continent of Mu
The Stone Tablets of Mu
Guy Needler
The History of God
Beyond the Source – Book 1,2
Avoiding Karma
Dee Wallace/Jarred Hewett
The Big E
Dee Wallace
Conscious Creation
Natalie Sudman
Application of Impossible Things
Henry Michaelson
And Jesus Said – A Conversation
Victoria Pendragon
SleepMagic
Riet Okken
The Liberating Power of Emotions
Janie Wells
Payment for Passage
Dennis Wheatley/ Maria Wheatley
The Essential Dowsing Guide
Dennis Milner
Kosmos
Garnet Schulhauser
Dancing on a Stamp
Julia Cannon
Soul Speak – The Language of Your Body
Charmian Redwood
Coming Home to Lemuria
Kathryn Andries
Soul Choices – 6 Paths to Find Your Life Purpose
Soul Choices – 6 Paths to Fulfilling Relationships
Kathryn & Patrick Andries
Naked in Public
Victoria Hunt
Kiss the Wind
Victor Parachin
Sit a Bit
Annie Stillwater Gray
Education of a Guardian Angel
Blair Styra
Don't Change the Channel
Sherry O'Brian
Peaks and Valleys: Integrative Approaches for Recovering from Loss
Sherry Wilde
The Forgotten Promise

For more information about any of the above titles, soon to be released titles, or other items in our catalog, write or visit our website:
PO Box 754, Huntsville, AR 72740
www.ozarkmt.com